THE PAST WITHIN US

THE PAST WITHIN US

An Empirical Approach
to Philosophy of History

BY RAYMOND MARTIN

Princeton University Press / Princeton, New Jersey

Copyright © 1989 by Princeton University Press
Published by Princeton University Press, 41 William Street
  Princeton, New Jersey 08540
In the United Kingdom: Princeton University Press,
  Oxford

Library of Congress Cataloging-in-Publication Data

Martin, Raymond, 1941–
    The past within us.

    Bibliography: p.
    Includes index.
    1. History—Philosophy.   I. Title.
D16.8.M2935   1989   901   88–32244
ISBN 0-691-07341-4

Publication of this book has been aided by grants from the
University of Maryland and the Paul Mellon Fund of
Princeton University Press
This book has been composed in Merganthaler Baskerville

Printed in the United States of America by
Princeton University Press, Princeton, New Jersey

To my Parents,

Louis and Ann Martin,

with love and gratitude

CONTENTS

PREFACE

ANALYTIC philosophy of history arose primarily in the twentieth century, and more or less self-consciously, as a reaction to other ways of doing philosophy of history. During what I shall call its "classic period," roughly the forty-year period from about 1935 to 1975, it developed a strong sense of its own identity and two persistent and closely related preoccupations: objectivity, perhaps the dominant preoccupation at the beginning of this period, and explanation, clearly the dominant preoccupation at the end.

Although analytic philosophers are still making significant contributions to philosophy of history, the rate of contributions has dropped sharply since the mid–1960s, and there is less commitment now to a common research program.[1] Other approaches to philosophy of history, nourished by other traditions, particularly a post-structuralist concern with narrative form, have rushed in to fill the void.[2] Currently, it is almost as if analytic philosophy of history, having completed one major phase of its development, is gathering its energy to enter another. The main purpose of the present book is to suggest a direction for it to take.

My point of departure will be a diagnosis of what I take to be an essential flaw in analytic philosophy of history during its classic period. This flaw is that analytic philosophers tended to give their highest priority to conceptual analysis and to consideration of what is possible in principle, rather than to an examination of historical studies themselves and to reflection on what is in fact the case. They often did this under the influence of the mistaken belief that conceptual analysis is more significant methodologically for historical studies than it actually is. The result was a kind of strategic withdrawal from the data that it is philosophy's main task to illuminate.[3]

My diagnosis of this flaw does not amount to a history of analytic philosophy of history. Far from it. There are many philosophers who have made a significant impact on the analytic debates—R. G. Collingwood, Maurice Mandelbaum, Isaiah Berlin, W. H. Walsh, Michael Scriven, Alan Donagan, and Arthur Danto, to mention just a few—whose works receive little or no discussion in what follows.[4] My objective is not to *do* history but rather to *use* history in order to make a methodological point about philosophy of history.

Instead of surveying the important work, I focus on just a few highly influential philosophers and a few key issues to try to capture something that has been central to the analytic approach. In this way, I hope to convey what I consider to be representative of what was going on in the field generally. By keeping the discussion uncluttered in this way, I hope to bring the main methodological point that I want to make into bold relief. That point has two sides. The critical side is my diagnosis of past errors. The constructive side is my sketch of what I hope is a better approach. This better approach has always been an aspect of analytic philosophy of history, but it has been relegated to a subordinate role and is often used to accomplish ends to which it is ill suited. Thus, the constructive side of my point is that we modify the order of our traditional priorities, and that we get clearer about what we should be doing and why.

Although this book is not an introductory book and is addressed primarily to philosophers of history, I have tried to make my discussion accessible to anyone who is interested in philosophy of history, regardless of background. What I have to say may be of most interest to those who are already familiar with the history of analytic philosophy of history and who have some curiosity about whether its traditional research programs can or should be revitalized. But I also hope that non-analytic philosophers, historians, and students of philosophy and history will find this book interesting and useful.

To this end, I have kept my discussion of key issues as simple as possible, concentrating just on what seems most central to the main points I want to make, and I have explained these points and my reasons for them in familiar, everyday language and with a non-analytic audience in mind. It should also help that my constructive proposals, if adopted, would result in a kind of analytic philosophy of history that is close to the earth and that has methodological significance for historical studies.

We are all historians, and I am ultimately concerned with understanding philosophically the role that our activity as historians plays in our everyday lives. But, after glancing briefly at such broader concerns, I focus primarily on the work of professional historians, a group that is understood to include not only historians proper, but also archaeologists and other professionals concerned with interpreting the past. The reason for this narrower focus is that to answer many of the philosophical questions that I argue we should be asking, we have to first understand how history is done when it is done as carefully and reliably as we know how to do it.

Finally, to help neutralize a bias that is built into our language, I have used both masculine and feminine pronouns where traditional usage would sanction only masculine ones.

ACKNOWLEDGMENTS

Several previously published papers were revised for portions of this book. These papers include: "Historical Counterexamples and Sufficient Cause," *Mind* (1979); "History and Subjectivity," *Ratio* (1979); "Beyond Positivism: A Research Program for Philosophy of History," *Philosophy of Science* (1981); "Causes, Conditions and Causal Importance," *History and Theory* (1982); and "History and the Brewmaster's Nose," *Canadian Journal of Philosophy* (1985). Chapter 3 is a revised version of "Explanatory Controversy in Historical Studies. A Case Study: The Classic Maya Collapse," which appeared in a book edited by Peter van Inwagen, *Time and Cause*, copyright © 1980 by D. Reidel Publishing Company, Dordrecht, Holland.

Thanks again to James Celarier, Patricia Hunt, David Grimsted, Daniel Hausman, Inge Lembeck, Jerrold Levinson, Andrus Pork, Harper Pryor, and John Vollrath for commenting helpfully on these earlier papers.

Thanks also and especially to John Barresi, Bernard Berofsky, Daniel Kolak, Michael Slote, Fred Suppe, and Richard Vann, each of whom generously read an entire, earlier draft of the present book and made many perceptive criticisms and helpful suggestions. This book is much better because of their help and encouragement.

I am also grateful to the General Research Board of the University of Maryland for supporting my research.

THE PAST WITHIN US

Chapter 1

TWO APPROACHES TO
PHILOSOPHY OF HISTORY

Our past, it seems, is behind us: fixed, stable, and secure. Our future is not fixed, but open. We can know our past, but we can only speculate about our future. Our present, neither stable nor secure, constantly and swiftly recedes into the past. Only by interpreting the past, and then viewing the present through the lens of this interpretation, can we locate ourselves in a stable world. If we cannot know what we will be, and cannot directly interpret who we are, at least, it seems, we can know what we have been. And in knowing what we have been, we discover who we are.

One thing we are is historians. We not only interpret what we have been, we have a deep need to do so. Every reader of this book, from the time they acquire an awareness of themselves to the present moment, has constructed and continually revises a narrative account of his own personal past. We have also constructed and continually revise narrative accounts of various groups to which we belong, such as our families. These narrative accounts are largely the products of our deep need for an identity. And we, that is, the we who we take ourselves to be, are largely their products. Our interpretations construct us, as much as we them.

Our amateur activity of interpreting our personal and group histories shades off into the professional historian's activity of interpreting our collective histories. Both are motivated by *the basic questions of historical studies*: What happened? Why did it happen? What does it mean? The first question is a request for facts, the second for explanation, the third for meaning or significance. All historical accounts answer at least the first question. Minimally complete historical studies

3

answer also the second. Full-blooded historical interpretations answer all three.

Historical interpretations are inevitable, and they come before philosophy of history. There would be no philosophy of
history if there were not first historical interpretations. But
philosophy of history is equally inevitable. Once there are
historical interpretations, reflective people are *bound* to ask
philosophical questions about them: What are historical interpretations? Why do we interpret our past as we do, rather
than in some other way or not at all? What is the significance
of the fact that we interpret our past as we do? These are *the
basic questions of philosophy of history*. The first is a request for
facts, the second for explanation, and the third for meaning
or significance. No philosophy of history is complete unless
it answers all three.

Once we ask the basic questions of philosophy of history,
the past is no longer what it used to be—fixed, stable and
secure. Only what is behind us can be fixed or stable or secure. *Our* past is not behind us. There may be *a* past behind
us—we assume there is—and it may be what really happened.
But, from our present perspective, that past is gone. It left its
imprint on the present, but to the extent that we are ignorant
of what it was and how it left that imprint, it is not a usable
past. The usable past, *our* past, is embedded in our historical
interpretations. And these interpretations are within us. For
theoretical purposes, we distinguish between *the* past and *our*
past, between what really happened and our best interpretations of what really happened. For practical purposes, this
distinction collapses. We have no direct access to *the* past. We
have direct access only to the present and to *our* past, which
is an artifact of the present. We carry our past within us. Our
past—the past within us—and the procedures we use to construct it are the focus of the present book.

There are a profusion of different, and even incompatible,
ways in which we could interpret the past. We choose among
them. But on what basis? To what extent are these choices an
expression of personal or group subjective preference? To
what extent are they constrained by evidence and by the con-

ventions for interpreting evidence to which we subscribe?
Are there realistic alternatives to our conventions for interpreting evidence? If not, why not? If there are, what are they,
and why do we not adopt them?

How shall we answer these and related questions? The first
step, surely, is to examine historical interpretations with an
eye to exposing their evidential structure. To find out how,
and how much, historical interpretations are constrained by
evidential conventions, we have to look in detail at historical
interpretations. The more carefully we look, the less fixed the
past looks, and the less it looks like the source of stability and
security we would like it to be. So, while historical interpretation tends to give us a relatively stable world, philosophy of
history tends to take it away. This may be one reason—a
deep, underlying reason—why historians are so often hostile
to philosophy of history.

The present book does not answer the basic questions of
philosophy of history. It is, rather, largely a prolegomenon to
the sort of philosophy of history which I recommend. My
main goal is a programmatic one, more methodological than
substantive. It is to change the way we approach philosophy
of history. I shall try to do this first by diagnosing what I take
to be an essential flaw in the analytic approach to philosophy
of history during its classic period, and then by characterizing
and illustrating a better approach.

My diagnosis depends on seeing analytic philosophy of history during its classic period as heavily implicated in what I
shall call "the conceptual approach" to philosophy of history.
Philosophers of history following this approach have tried to
answer the basic questions of philosophy of history primarily
through conceptual analysis of the language of historical
studies. Their point of departure has been words—like "explanation," "cause," and "objectivity"—rather than the evidential structure of actual historical interpretations. As a
natural consequence, these philosophers have been primarily
concerned with what is possible in principle, rather than with
what is actual or with what is possible in fact. The legacy of
this approach still haunts the philosophy of history today.

The alternative that I favor is to drop our preoccupation with conceptual analysis and look instead at actual historical interpretations, with an eye to uncovering the evidential conventions in terms of which we construct them. To be realistic, as we shall see, this looking at historical interpretations must be done from a *comparative* perspective that takes seriously the limitations within which historians actually work; that is, it must be done from the perspective of trying to determine how historians try to show that their favored interpretations are *better* than competing interpretations. I shall call this alternative approach "the empirical approach" to philosophy of history. It is empiricial, in contrast to the traditional, conceptual approach, in that it takes its point of departure not from an analysis of concepts, but rather from an examination of facts, the most central of which are the ways historians argue that one interpretation is better than its competitors. The empirical approach offers not only a new way of addressing the basic questions of philosophy of history, but also a new understanding of the traditional, conceptual approach to philosophy of history.

We, analytic philosophers of history, have grown tired of our old debates, but we have not yet addressed the task of understanding philosophically why our old debates became tiresome. I shall argue that when we do understand what was wrong with the old debates, we shall be able to see why our traditional, conceptual approach to philosophy of history has not been well suited to answering the basic questions of philosophy of history. It will then be easier to see how we need to change our approach so that it is better suited. Thus, my explanation of what I take to be an essential flaw in the conceptual approach to philosophy of history is an important part of my argument for the empirical approach.

The analytic approach to philosophy of history arose largely in order to correct the deficiencies of still earlier approaches. It retained throughout its classic period a spirit of reform as well as an undisguised enthusiasm for conceptual analysis. Both are nicely captured in the opening paragraph of Morton White's widely read *The Foundations of Historical Knowledge*, published in 1965:

This is a study in the philosophy of history, a discipline with a
checkered past, a respectable present and, I hope, a brighter future. Once the philosophy of history was associated almost exclusively with grand speculation about the development of society,
with pretentious volumes on the laws of civilization and its decay,
and with futile debates about whether heroes, ideas, or material
circumstances alone shape the course of human history. . . . But
all of this has changed dramatically when philosophers—especially British and American philosophers—came to focus so much
of their attention on the logic of language, the method of science,
and the analysis of concepts. . . . Instead of seeking to chart the
development of epochs, cultures, and civilizations, the contemporary philosopher of history is more interested in analyzing historical thought and language. . . . [He is] anxious to elucidate terms
that are commonly employed by historians and historically
minded thinkers, and eager to advance toward a clearer understanding of the chief intellectual activities of the historian.[1]

White leaves so-called speculative philosophy of history behind and stresses the importance of understanding the chief
intellectual activities of the historian. It is hard to quarrel with
these objectives. But should "elucidating terms" be our primary vehicle to such understanding?

Speculative philosophy of history began perhaps with the
classical Greeks, certainly by the time of Augustine, and
reached its zenith in the powerful historical visions of Vico,
Hegel, and Marx. It arose, as all science arises, primarily from
the need for theoretical coherence. And it was in its time an
appropriate response to that need. At its best, it profoundly
affected our approach to the study of human behavior, and it
is still able to move us. But its time has passed, not for lack of
speculative genius, but rather because historical studies themselves have replaced it. Just as the natural sciences earlier
replaced theology as an intellectual discipline that could claim
seriously to provide knowledge of nature, so also historical
studies replaced speculative philosophy of history as a discipline that could claim seriously to provide knowledge of
human society. The process of replacement was gradual, but
by the end of the nineteenth century the transition was all but
complete. Spengler and Toynbee, writing in the twentieth cen-

tury, had almost no effect on either historical studies or philosophy.

Speculative philosophy of history, for all its majesty and insight and poetic vision, failed in the end because it had scientific pretensions but lacked both a scientific method and an adequate empirical base. Its practitioners characteristically made large-scale empirical claims, their so-called laws of historical development, which always suffered from one or another of two fatal defects: either they were too vague to be evaluated by appeal to empirical evidence, or else they were specific enough to be evaluated and could be shown to be false. With the professionalization of historical studies, historians restricted themselves to clearer claims and more modest objectives.

Speculative philosophy of history gave way to so-called critical philosophy of history, which was fully born in Vico's work in the early eighteenth century, but which did not begin in earnest or as a corporate enterprise until the latter part of the nineteenth century. Critical philosophy of history had to await the professionalization of historical studies. Just as speculative philosophy of history was possible as a serious intellectual discipline only before the professionalization of historical studies, so also critical philosophy of history was possible only after it.

The key question for critical philosophers of history has always been, and perhaps always will be, the question of how to resolve the tension between scientific and humanistic approaches to the study of human behavior. One might say that the question of how this tension should be resolved has been the main issue for critical philosophy of history. That would be true, but it would be an understatement. It is closer to the truth, if a slight overstatement, to say that it has been the only issue.

Analytic philosophy of history—the primary form that critical philosophy of history has taken in the British and American tradition—has twice gathered itself around a central problem. The first time, in the 1930s, 1940s, and 1950s, the problem was objectivity. The second time, in the 1950s, 1960s, and 1970s, the problem was explanation. During each of these periods there was a prolonged debate, sometimes fierce, at the root of which was the perennial tension between scientific and humanistic approaches to the study of human behavior.

The basis for the first debate, over objectivity, was laid toward the end of the nineteenth century by American disciples of the German historian, Leopold von Ranke. These historians advocated an approach to historical studies that was born of respect for scientific methodology and nurtured by humility. This approach was, in effect, a retreat from the pretentious search for generalizations and laws toward a kind of scientific historiography that would devote itself exclusively to the discovery of facts.

These early positivists were answered in the United States by Carl Becker and Charles Beard. Both Becker and Beard called upon their fellow historians to cast off this suffocating ideal of a scientific historiography and to face up to the radically humanistic and relativistic character of their discipline. At about the same time, in Germany, the sociologist Karl Mannheim was also arguing forcefully for a relativistic account of historical studies. The fusion of these two sources of subjectivistic arguments provoked a philosophical literature on the possibility of objectivity in historical studies. My main concern in Chapter 5 is with the approach to the question of historical objectivity which is found in this philosophical literature.[2] I explain why this approach, arguably still the dominant one in analytic circles, has outlived its usefulness. Then, in Chapter 6, I illustrate what I hope is a better approach.

The basis for the second analytic debate, over explanation, was laid in the 1930s and 1940s, also in America, and also by positivists, but this time primarily by philosophers, as a by-product of the philosophical maturation of Logical Positivist philosophy of science. The approach of these later positivists, also born of respect for science but this time nurtured by audacity, grew into a call for a more scientific historiography that would appreciate the ubiquity and centrality of explanations in historical accounts and acknowledge the obligation to back up these explanations with a search for generalizations and historical laws.

The philosophy of science from which this later positivistic view of historical studies sprang provoked its most profound reaction in the 1960s and 1970s in the relativistic subjectivism of Thomas Kuhn. But Kuhn's focus was on science and its history, not on philosophy of history. Within philosophy of history, the most visible and influential reaction was perhaps that of William Dray, who developed a view which might be called "evaluative subjectivism."

It is curious that the earlier and later positivist initiatives, each of which provoked a long debate, advocated seemingly incompatible methodological recommendations: in the first case to eschew generalizations and laws, in the second to pursue them. These recommendations are not strictly incompatible because the two groups of positivists had different sorts of generalizations and laws in mind. The earlier positivists were trying to separate themselves from a historiography that appealed to grand laws of historical development such as are found in their most pretentious form in speculative philosophies of history. The later positivists had no sympathy with grand laws of historical development or with speculative philosophies of history, but advocated instead the modestly theoretical approach of academic social science. Even so, the two positivist recommendations are discordant. What makes them both positivist recommendations is that the ideal of historical methodology to which they appeal is scientific methodology, or what they take to be scientific methodology, and their methodological recommendations are based on the conviction that historians ought to imitate this scientific methodology as closely as they can within the limitations of historical studies.

The opponents of these two groups of positivists are usually lumped together under the negative label, "anti-positivists." I shall call these antipositivists, "humanists," because they shared a common concern for defending the methodological autonomy of "the humanities." What the humanists had in common was partly the belief that historical methodology is autonomous and inherently subjective, but mostly the shared feeling that the specific methodological recommendations that were being urged in the name of a scientific historiography were inappropriate. It is as if the humanists responded to the positivists by saying, "If this is what it means to do history scientifically, and hence objectively, we choose to do history humanistically, and hence subjectively." Whereas the positivists in each case, and more or less as a group, urged a specific set of methodological recommendations, the humanists had no alternative set of shared methodological recommendations. Each humanist, so far as constructive recommendations were concerned, was an island unto himself.

Although these two main debates within analytic philosophy of history have subsided, the central issues that provoked them were never resolved. They subsided not because the philosophical questions they addressed got answered to the satisfaction of most philosophers of history, but rather because the way these questions were debated became redundant and tiresome. They ended when it became increasingly clear that continuing these debates on the same basis was not going to shed more light on the basic questions of philosophy of history.

But what was the matter with the way the old debates were structured? Philosophers of history, curiously enough, have taken little interest in answering this question and thereby revealing the philosophical significance of the fact that our main debates became sterile. Why have we not been more interested? Partly, no doubt, because so little time has elapsed since these debates have subsided—particularly the debate over explanation—that until recently we have not been able to see these debates whole. But probably the main reason we have not been more interested, ironically, is that we just have not seen that there is something philosophically interesting to learn from our own history.

I shall argue that the main problem with these debates over explanation and objectivity is that both positivists and humanists shared certain assumptions which drew attention away from the examination of actual historical interpretations. These assumptions were false. But the debates became tiresome not so much because these assumptions were false, but primarily because they were sterile. Conducting the debates on the basis of these assumptions virtually guaranteed that we would never advance far toward answering the basic questions of philosophy of history.

The underlying problem was that both the positivists and the humanists tended to work within the framework of the conceptual approach to philosophy of history. Within this framework questions about historical studies were routinely formulated as questions about the language of historical studies, answered a priori, and then the answers were used as a basis for making methodological recommendations about how actual history should be done. So, for instance, philosophers did conceptual philosophy of history when they converted questions about explanation or objectivity into questions about the concepts of explanation or objectivity, attempted to answer these latter questions a priori, and then used the answers as a basis for methodological recommendations.

The conceptual approach tends to become sterile largely because it treats our current ideas—of explanation, of objectivity, and so on—as if they were simpler and more worthy of respect than they are. Simpler because it treats them as if they were more uniform than they are, as if there were just one or a few core ideas of each notion which we could capture in an explicit formula. More worthy of respect because it treats these ideas as if their status as our current ideas confers upon them a sort of timeless legitimacy. But it does not. We can analyze language and construct models a priori as much as we like. Whether it is fruitful to apply these analyses and models to a given domain and in what ways it is fruitful to do so will remain empirical issues. An analogy may help to make this point clear.

Scientists often construct theoretical models by defining a priori the properties of ideal systems. This is sensible scientific practice. But it is always an open question whether the ideal systems so defined are applicable to the real world, and their applicability can only be determined empirically. For instance, one can construct an a priori model of a "Newtonian Particle System" by defining it as a system that satisfies Newton's three laws of motion and the law of universal gravitation. But it would not follow from having so defined this model that any actual system—say, our solar system—is a Newtonian Particle System. Whether some actual system is a Newtonian Particle System can only be determined empirically. Thus, when Edmund Halley, operating on the hypothesis that our solar system is a Newtonian Particle System, predicted in 1705 the return in December of 1758 of a comet, there could be no a priori guarantee that his prediction would come true. The fact that it did come true was evidence that our solar system is a Newtonian Particle System.[3]

The point of this analogy is simply that we must always question whether our concepts and models—whether based on traditional linguistic practice or newly minted does not matter—are the right concepts or models for the particular problem at hand. There can be no a priori guarantee that they will be.

Those who follow the conceptual approach to philosophy of history tend to forget that the immediate point of historical studies is to formulate interpretations that solve specific historiographical problems. Hence the point of departure for deciding which concepts and models would be useful has to be the problems that these concepts and models are being used to solve.

Only an examination of the historiographical problem under consideration, and of its internal dynamics, can answer whether a concept or model has a useful role to play in solving a problem. And not all historiographical problems are the same. Thus, there is bound to be some variation regarding which concepts and models are going to be useful. The point is not "anything goes" in the process of historical interpretation, but rather what goes depends importantly on where it is going and on the idiosyncratic constraints of the journey. It is not useful to determine where a historical interpretation should go, or how it should get there, before carefully considering the particular historiographical problem to be solved and the practical limitations that constrain our attempts to solve it.

There is no denying that conceptual analysis can sometimes be useful. But conceptual analysis is not the most productive point of departure for finding out what we most need to know to answer the basic questions of philosophy of history. Rather, the most productive points of departure are historical interpretations and ongoing historiographical controversies.

Admittedly, the contrast I am drawing between conceptual and empirical approaches to philosophy of history is an idealization. No philosopher ever followed the conceptual approach unflinchingly, totally unresponsive to the empirical realities of the data he was trying to explain. No philosopher ever could or should follow an empirical approach that is not importantly influenced by conceptual considerations. The issue is one of emphasis. Nevertheless, a relatively sharp contrast between these two approaches is a useful point of departure for understanding why the traditional analytic approach has not been more fruitful in answering the basic questions of philosophy of history. This initial sharp contrast between conceptual and empirical approaches will be replaced in the chapters to follow by more fine-grained distinctions.

The attitudes I have described as characteristic of the conceptual approach are quintessentially positivist attitudes. They were, and still would be, rejected by most humanists. But the humanists, as we shall see, came under the influence of the conceptual approach not only by allowing the positivists to set the agenda for philosophical discussion, but also by restructuring their own positions so as to bring them into direct *conceptual* conflict with the positivist positions.

Analytic philosophy of history is currently at a crossroad. The traditional debates over objectivity and explanation have run out of steam. A new focus has not yet arrived to replace them. And while it is clear that analytic philosophers of history will continue to discuss the basic questions of philosophy of history, still fueled by the tension between scientific and humanistic approaches to the study of human behavior, it is not yet clear how they will do so.[4] The point of the present book is to suggest a new way to approach these basic questions, a way that transcends both positivism and its humanistic alternatives. The empirical approach does not do away with the tension between scientific and humanistic approaches. Rather, it expresses this tension within the framework of a new set of categories and a new research program, both of

which take their point of departure from an examination of
the evidential structure of actual historical interpretations.
Past failures and future prospects are inextricably linked.
The best way to understand the empirical approach, and not
just why it is necessary, is to understand what is wrong with
the main approach followed previously. And the best way to
understand this old approach is to view it from the perspective of the empirical approach. I turn now to this dual project.

Chapter 2

POSITIVISM AND ITS CRITICS:
THE COMMON ASSUMPTIONS

Carl hempel's classic paper, "The Function of General Laws in History," published in 1942, launched a debate that lasted over thirty years. During this time philosophy of history became virtually a one-issue field. That issue was historical explanation. There was more written on historical explanation during this period than in all previous history. Unfortunately, the energy invested in this debate paid few dividends for philosophy of history. Historical explanation was not explored primarily on its own terms, by looking at actual historical explanations, but rather by way of debating the merits of the positivist theory of historical explanation. And this debate, for reasons I shall explain, tended to draw attention away from the examination of historical explanation rather than toward it.

Why then did Hempel's paper and the positivist theory of historical explanation which it proposed attract so much interest? There are different answers for the different groups that were party to the debate. Positivist philosophers of science who had no special interest in historical explanation for its own sake felt compelled to show that a theory of explanation which they claimed was applicable to the natural sciences was applicable also to the social sciences and to historical studies. Prima facie historical explanation fit the theory least. But allowing historical explanation as an exception did not mean simply that the positivist theory could not be defended as a general theory of explanation. It also cast doubt on its adequacy even as an account of scientific explanation. The reason is that the positivist theory was defended primarily a priori on the basis of a philosophical analysis, that is, a reductive definition, of what it means for something to be an explanation. If historical explanations were allowed as an exception, then the positivist analysis could not be defended as an analysis of what it means for something to be an explanation per se. The positivist analysis might still have been defended simply as an analysis of what it means for something to be a scientific explanation. But such a qualification would have put a strain on the positivist emphasis on "unity of science," and it would have been tricky to draw the line between scientific and non-scientific explanations.

Philosophers of history and philosophically minded historians were interested in the positivist theory primarily because it was usually proposed and defended as a theory that had important methodological implications. Even humanists, as we shall see, invariably shared the assumption that it had important methodological implications. Thus it was possible to appeal to the positivist theory, and many did appeal to it, to argue that historians do history differently—"more scientifically" than many historians were trained or inclined to do it. Humanistic critics of a "more scientific" history, convinced that these methodological recommendations were a mistake, felt obligated to show that the analysis that seemed to imply them was also a mistake.

The strictly philosophical debate over the positivist theory of explanation coincided with a closely related debate already dividing historians. This intrahistorical debate, a version of the perennial tension between science and the humanities, was between historians oriented in the social sciences, on the one hand, and more traditionally oriented historians, on the other, and it was explicitly a methodological debate. Historians oriented in the social sciences were urging that history be done more quantitatively, within a framework that was sensitive to social science theory, and with an eye toward some sort of generalizable results. Traditionally oriented historians were resisting these suggestions. The discipline of history itself was in the throes of an identity crisis. The positivist analysis of historical explanation was seen to support historians oriented in the social sciences, and thus added fuel to this crisis. Thus, many historians who otherwise would have had little interest in philosophical debates got interested in this one.

In the end, the question of most interest to philosophers of history and philosophically minded historians was the question of how historical explanations ought to be defended. A great deal has now been written on this topic, so much in fact that it is natural to suppose that scholarly industry has long since exhausted it of whatever philosophical or methodological interest it may once have had. Nothing could be further from the truth. Debate over the positivist theory made quite a limited contribution to our understanding of how historical explanations should be defended. The main reason is that certain mistaken assumptions were tacitly accepted both by positivists and their humanist critics. Because of these mistaken assumptions, the debate was conducted in a way that drew attention away from the examination of actual historical explanations, and thus the debate was too far removed from the realities of explanatory controversy in historical studies to shed much light on how historical explanations should be defended.

These mistaken assumptions that were shared by both positivists and humanists concern the relationship between the positivist analysis and the questions, first, of how historians should defend their explanations, and secondly, of when historians are rationally entitled to prefer one explanation to another. I can best explain these assumptions, and also illustrate how they lay beneath the surface of the debate and influenced its direction, by characterizing briefly two well-known positivist accounts of how historical explanations should be defended. In my opinion, the methodological recommendations suggested in these accounts are badly mistaken. But it is not my primary purpose to criticize these recommendations. There exists already a large critical literature. My purpose, rather, is to expose certain hitherto unnoticed assumptions that lie behind these recommendations, and that were tacitly accepted both by positivists and their critics. To understand why the debate over the positivist theory made such a limited contribution to our understanding of historical explanation we must see not only what these assumptions were but also how they were embedded in and influenced the debate.

Consider first Morton White's well-known elaboration and defense of the positivist theory in *Foundations of Historical Knowledge*. The emphasis in White's account is on the analysis of historical explanation, rather than on the question of how historical explanations should be defended. The latter question is hardly discussed at all—mainly in only eight continuous pages. White's neglect of methodological issues is symptomatic of the shared assumption that if the positivist analysis of historical explanation is true, then the question of how historians should defend the explanations they propose is thereby all but settled.

White's eight-page discussion of the question of how historical explanations should be defended is devoted to an objection by the Dutch historian Pieter Geyl to Arnold Toynbee's claim that "the prosperity and cultural fecundity" (Geyl's words) of Holland during a certain period of its history was due to the response of its people to the harsh challenge of the sea. Geyl claimed that

> within the European and even within the Netherlands cultural areas the rise of Holland was fairly late, and this no doubt as a result of these very conditions created by sea and rivers. If in the end it overcame these conditions, it was not without the assistance of the surrounding higher forms of civilization (even the Romans and their dyke-building had an important share in making the region habitable). But can, even after that initial stage, the continued struggle with the water be decisive in explaining the later prosperity and cultural fecundity of the country? Is it not indispensable to mention the excellence of the soil, once it had become possible to make use of it? and above all the situation, which promoted the rise of shipping and of a larger international commerce? Was the case of Holland then wholly due to hard conditions after all?[1]

Geyl obviously thinks that his explanation of the prosperity and cultural fecundity of Holland during the period in question, to the extent he offers an explanation, is *more nearly* sufficient than Toynbee's explanation. But there is nothing to warrant the assumption that Geyl thinks his explanation is sufficient. Nevertheless, White attributes to Geyl the implicit claim that Geyl's explanation is sufficient by attributing to him the claim that Holland "achieved success *because of* . . . the challenge of the sea, the excellence of Holland's soil, the assistance of the surrounding forms of civilization, and the maritime situation of Holland."[2] White may have been motivated to recast Geyl's claim by the fact that the positivist analysis is most applicable to explanations claimed to be sufficient. Whatever the reason, the claim White attributes to Geyl is stronger than any Geyl actually makes, and this stronger claim is one that would be near impossible for Geyl to justify. Probably that is why Geyl was wise enough not to make it.

Having attributed to Geyl the claim that his explanation is sufficient, White next argues that Geyl can defend his explanation only if he can defend some such generalization as (G): "whenever a nation is subjected to the challenge of the sea, has excellent soil, is assisted by its neighbors, and has an excellent maritime situation, it will rise to great heights of success." Then White specifies the ways that are available to Geyl to defend (G). White concedes that there may well be just one instance of (G), the very case under examination. Hence, if Geyl's ability to defend his explanation depends on his ability to defend (G) by citing several instances of (G), he cannot defend (G) and cannot defend his explanation. But White argues that there are two other ways to defend a generalization.

The first way is to deduce the generalization from other well-confirmed generalizations. White illustrates this way by imagining that the inventor of the match, just after he got the first one to light, claimed that "it lit because it was dry and struck in the presence of oxygen." White claims that the match man could have defended the generalization, "any dry match when struck in the presence of oxygen will light," by deducing it from chemical laws concerning the behavior of sulphur and the statement that matches are made of sulphur. Perhaps so. But there is nothing available to Geyl that is even remotely analogous to chemical laws from which he might deduce (G).

The second way of defending generalizations is inductive. White imagines that Hume explained why Adam Smith did not on a certain occasion stab Hume to rob him of his silver standish by citing the information that Smith was honest and opulent, had lived for years in intimate friendship with Hume, and on the occasion in question had been in Hume's house only while Hume was surrounded by his servants. White explains that Hume could have defended his *explanation* by appealing to the generalization, "For any pair of individuals x and y, if x is honest and opulent, and x and y had lived for years in intimate friendship, and x comes into the house of y, and y is surrounded by his servants, then x does not stab y in order to rob y of y's standish." Then White claims that Hume could have defended this *generalization* by arguing

> that honest men usually do not rob, that opulent men usually do not rob, that friends usually do not stab one, that people usually do not attack one in the presence of one's servants. Hume could have said that all of these facts together supply evidence for the *law* that no opulent, honest friend would ever stab one in the presence of one's servants in order to rob one, using the argument that if each of these considerations points strongly to the conclusion, all of them together make it certain.[3]

But even if White is right—which is doubtful—that Hume could have defended his generalization in this way, Geyl could not have defended (G) in an analogous way. Countries that have either excellent soil or the assistance of surrounding forms of civilization or an excellent maritime situation do not usually exhibit those aspects of the prosperity and cultural fecundity of Holland during the period in question that it was Geyl's objective to explain.

The remainder of White's discussion implies that most of the explanations proposed by historians are not justified and that the only way for historians to improve this deplorable situation is for them to justify generalizations that at least approximate those covering generalizations that underlie their explanations. White writes:

> I repeat, however, that if, after a regularist transforms Geyl's explanation of the rise of Holland into a deductive argument whose generalization applies to only one example, and the generalization is not given the sort of extra boost that the match man can give

his or that Hume can give his, then the generalization is in trouble—*and so is Geyl's explanation.* It makes no difference that a historian should believe such an explanation with confidence if he cannot do more to support it. . . . So far, then, from presenting an otiose account of historical explanation, the regularist may bring home to the historian the fragility of some of his explanations.[4]

White concludes by insisting that "historical explanations are, in general, more tenuously constructed, more debatable, [and] more subject to doubt than the explanations of natural scientists." He claims it is a virtue of his account to have revealed why this is so.

Murray Murphey, in *Our Knowledge of the Historical Past,* published in 1973, is even tougher than White. Murphey accepts White's basic analysis of historical explanation, but warns historians that this analysis

> does not legitimize the current practice of presenting singular causal statements only and ignoring general laws. The historian is responsible for the truth of the statements which his history contains. No historian would hazard a non-causal factual statement without citing evidence to support it. Similarly, *he must present evidence to support his causal statements, and the only way he can present such evidence is to exhibit the covering law in question.*[5]

White's implicit suggestion that historians ought to back up their causal explanations with generalizations which approximate appropriate covering laws becomes in Murphey's account the explicit recommendation that historians ought to formulate and defend the covering laws themselves. To make matters worse, Murphey adds that unless a historian can justify a covering law for his explanation, then his "putative explanation remains conjectural only."[6]

Clearly something has gone wrong. White's and Murphey's recommendations are wildly implausible. Even the best historians do not follow them, and it is difficult to believe they should. It would be ludicrous of Geyl, for example, to attempt to defend his explanation by attempting to justify (G). The main thing we would expect from Geyl, were his criticism of Toynbee sufficiently controversial that he felt obligated to argue for it, is an argument that his explanation is *better* than

Toynbee's explanation. Geyl could not show this by attempting to justify (G). The reason, as White showed convincingly, is that there is not much Geyl could do to defend (G). But Geyl could defend the comparative superiority of his explanation, among other ways, by arguing that Toynbee's explanation is insufficient and that each of the factors that Geyl mentions in his own explanation contributed to the financial and cultural prosperity of Holland. It would be easy, for instance, for Geyl to produce evidence—say, in part by documenting the financial success of agriculture in Holland during the period in question—that excellent soil contributed to the financial and cultural prosperity of Holland.

What led White and Murphey astray? The humanists routinely assumed, and still do, that what led the positivists astray and hence led to such implausible accounts of how historians ought to defend their explanations is that the positivist *analysis* of historical explanation is mistaken. Thus, the humanists spent a major portion of their energy trying to refute the positivist analysis. But they were never able to show convincingly that the crucial part of the positivist analysis—the claim that sufficient causal explanations imply the existence of at least probabilistic covering generalizations—is mistaken. No humanist argument to show this ever won general acceptance even among the humanists. The reason, I believe, why the humanists were unable to show that this central core of the positivist analysis is mistaken is simply that, given our current understanding of what counts as an explanation, it is not mistaken, at least in its application to historical explanation. I explain why in the Appendix. The important point for present purposes is that the humanists, by repeatedly attacking the positivist analysis without ever convincingly defeating it, merely added fuel to the debate, prolonging it for decades and often even obscuring aspects of historical methodology which support the positivist analysis. Worst of all, in focusing on the positivist analysis, they all but turned away from the detailed examination of actual explanatory controversy in historical studies.

Ironically, what led White and Murphey astray is the same thing that led the humanists astray: two undefended assumptions which underlay virtually all positivist accounts and which were accepted routinely by both positivists and humanists. The first assumption is this:

> (1) If the positivist analysis of historical explanation is correct, then historians ought to attempt to defend covering laws, or generalizations which closely approximate covering laws, for each of the explanations they propose.[7]

The second assumption is this:

> (2) Unless a historian can justify an explanation that he proposes, then his preference for that explanation is not rationally defensible.

Assumption (1) is implicit in White's account and explicit in Murphey's account. Assumption (2) is just beneath the surface in both accounts. Assumption (2) is implicit, for instance, in White's insistence that unless Geyl can justify his explanation, his explanation is "in trouble," and in Murphey's claim that unless a historian can justify his explanation, his explanation "remains conjectural only."

White and Murphey could assume (1) and (2) without defending them because their humanist critics also assumed them. Indeed, most humanists seem to have attacked the positivist analysis of historical explanation largely because they shared these assumptions but could not accept that historians ought to defend covering laws for each of the explanations they propose or they could not defend their explanations. An unfortunate consequence of the widespread tacit acceptance of these assumptions was that debate over how historians ought to defend their explanations inevitably tended to shift away from the detailed examination of actual controversies over explanation in historical studies and toward argument over the adequacy of the positivist analysis of historical explanation.

Assumption (1) is false. It says that if the positivist analysis is correct, then historians ought to attempt to defend at least probabilistic covering laws for each explanation they propose. But a historian may be able to show that his favored explanation is *better than* the best competing explanations without defending a covering law for it. This often happens, as, for instance, in the case of Geyl's explanation, when the historian's attempt to justify a covering law for his favored explanation, were he to make such an attempt, would be a manifest failure. It also happens when the historian is able to justify, to whatever extent, a covering law for his favored explanation, but covering laws could be justified for the best competing explanations. In such circumstances it is usually pointless for the historian to attempt to justify a covering law for his favored explanation. Since scholarly time and energy are limited resources, it is often worse than pointless, it is counterproductive. Thus, *whether or not* the positivist analysis of historical explanation is correct, it is false that historians ought always to attempt to justify covering laws for their favored explanations.

One might object that whether or not historians ought actually to attempt to justify covering laws for their explanations, they ought not to propose explanations unless they could, if challenged, justify covering laws for them. But there is abundant historiographical evidence that historians often cannot justify covering laws for explanations that they nevertheless can show are better than the best competing explanations. A number of examples will be provided in this book. Admittedly, a historian must have reason to think that the facts mentioned in his explanation are relevant to what he is attempting to explain. But he can have reason to think so without being better able to justify an appropriate covering law than, say, Geyl is in the example discussed by White. Anyone who doubts this should reflect on the example of competing explanations of the entry of the United States into World War I. Thus, the recommendation that historians ought not to propose explanations unless they could, if challenged, justify covering laws for them would gratuitously require historians to tell us less than they know and less than their readers wish to learn from them.

A historian who can show that his favored explanation of some significant historical event is better than the best competing explanations has knowledge that others value, whether or not he is able to justify a covering law for his explanation

and even whether or not his explanation is supported by
substantial evidence. Thus, it is a commonplace of historiography that historians will continue to debate the relative merits of competing explanations of some significant historical
event even though none of the competing explanations is
supported by substantial evidence.

The problem with (2) is that if a historian can justify an
explanation only if he can justify a covering law for it, then
(2) is also false. A historian can show that his preference for
an explanation is rationally defensible merely by showing that
his favored explanation is better than the best competing explanation. And he can often do that even though he cannot
justify a covering law for his favored explanation. Thus, if the
positivists are right that a historian can justify an explanation
only if he can justify a covering law for it, then a historian can
sometimes show that his preference for an explanation is
rationally defensible even though he cannot justify that explanation.

One might object that if the best that historians normally
can do to defend their explanations is to show that they are
better than the best competing explanations, then historians
ought to restrict the claims they make on behalf of their explanations. For instance, historians ought never to claim that
their explanations are justified or probably true, but only that
they are *better* justified or *more* probably true than the best
competing explanations. But this objection is irrelevant to the
question at issue, which is a methodological one. The objection has implications only for what historians should say
about the explanations they defend. While this is an important consideration, it has no implications for how historians
should defend their explanations.

I am not proposing a criterion of my own for "justification"
or "rational belief" or "historical knowledge." In particular, I
am not proposing that an explanation is justified per se just
in case it is better supported by the available evidence than is
every competing explanation. I believe that it is largely because philosophers have been preoccupied with such criteria
that their accounts of how historians should defend their explanations are often so unrealistic. Judging from the way his-

torians actually defend their explanations, their functional objective is to show that their favored explanations are better than the best competing explanations. It is this objective that determines what strategies historians employ to defend their explanations.

While the best historians almost always attempt to show, and often succeed in showing, that their explanations are better than the best competing explanations, they rarely attempt to show that their explanations are sufficient or that there are justified covering laws for their explanations.[8] They apparently believe that if they did attempt to show these things, they would seldom succeed in showing them or in strengthening their arguments for the comparative superiority of their favored explanations. The extent to which this apparent belief is correct can be determined only on a case-by-case basis. However, the important point is that it does not matter for the purpose of determining how a historian should defend his favored explanation whether his defense will show that his explanation is justified per se or rationally believable or known to be true. Historians can happily leave such questions to philosophers. Historians are rarely able to do more in defense of their controversial explanations of historical events than to show that they are better than the best competing explanations. But that is enough.

The question of how historians should defend the explanations they propose is a good question for the philosophy of history. It is of methodological interest to historians and of epistemological interest to philosophers. But we have seen that whether or not the positivist analysis is correct makes little difference to our understanding of how historians should defend their explanations. The only appropriate way to answer the question of how historians should defend their explanations is to begin by characterizing the ways in which explanatory claims are actually defended in the best historical work that is available. Such a characterization would reveal what immediate objectives historians pursue when they attempt to defend their explanations and what conceptual and evidential limitations limit their attempts to achieve these objectives. Despite a vast amount of philosophical literature on historical explanation, work on this program has barely begun. Yet philosophers will never be able to say how historians should defend their explanations unless they know what objectives historians pursue, how they try to achieve these objectives, and what alternative means are available to achieve them. The latter can only be known on a case-by-case basis. Thus, it is difficult to see how there can ever be adequate grounds for general prescriptions—such as those of White and Murphey—about how historians should defend their explanations.

It would be surprising if the ways in which explanations are actually defended in the best available historical work could not be improved upon. There is always room for improvement, in every field of inquiry. However, it would be just as surprising if the ways in which explanations are actually defended in the best historical work are not fairly close to the ways in which they should be defended. The best historical work, after all, is done by the best historians. And the best historians are those who are most competent to write history. Thus, until philosophers characterize the ways in which explanations are actually defended in the best historical work that is available, they will lack a basis for making realistic proposals concerning how historians should defend their explanations. Unrealistic proposals, such as those of White and Murphey, merely reinforce the widespread and substantially justified belief among practicing historians that the work done over decades in the philosophy of history on the justification of historical explanation is largely irrelevant to their professional objectives.

I have claimed, in this chapter, that controversial explanations in the best historical work available are almost invariably defended by means of arguments designed to show that the favored explanation is better than the best competing explanations. If this claim is correct, then the attempt to characterize the ways in which good historians defend their explanations gives rise immediately to two second-order problems. The first is to clarify the notion of "competing explanation." The second is to formulate adequate criteria for determining which of two competing explanations is better. Philosophers of history have not addressed the first of these problems, and only recently have begun to address the second. Other second-order problems also arise. I do not know what all of these problems are or what the solutions to any of them are. However, I do claim that the question of how historians should defend their explanations is alive and well and that the obvious way to begin to answer the question is with a careful look at the ways in which good historians actually defend their explanations. But that is all we need to know for now. The only practical question is what to do next.

Chapter 3

EXPLANATORY COMPETITION

T HE PROBLEM of explaining the collapse in the ninth century A.D. of the Classic Period Lowland Maya civilization is among the most celebrated puzzles of archaeology. In the present chapter, I want to use the controversy over how to solve this problem to begin the process of explaining how historians—including archaeologists as well as historians proper—defend their explanations.

It may seem to those familiar with the voluminous literature on historical explanation that philosophers have already described the strategies historians employ to defend their explanations. They have not.[1] The main reason for this is that philosophers giving an account of historical explanation have been until recently preoccupied with the positivist theory of historical explanation, and that theory motivates a non-comparative theory of explanatory justification. The positivist theory focuses on the question of what it takes to show that an explanation is sufficient. It does not speak directly to the question of what it takes to show that one explanation, whether partial or sufficient, is better than another. Yet historians almost always defend their explanations in a comparative way, that is, by attempting to show that their explanations are better than the competition. They are rarely able to show, and seldom claim to show, that their explanations are sufficient. Hence, philosophical accounts of what it takes to show that an explanation is sufficient are usually far removed from actual explanatory controversy in historical studies. As a natural consequence, historians often reject such accounts as unrecognizable from the viewpoint of historical practice.

30

The overriding explanatory objective of historians is to show that their explanations are better than competing explanations, and they attempt to do this by arguing both *for* their explanations and *against* competing explanations. Thus, there is a better way to look at the question of how historians defend their explanations than through the lens of the positivist theory. That is to understand how historians actually attempt to show and sometimes succeed in showing that their explanations, whether partial or sufficient, are better justified, or more generally better, than competing explanations. Realistic methodological recommendations about how historians should defend their explanations must be based on an understanding of the strategies historians actually employ to defend their explanations and of the constraints under which they work.

The Classic Period Lowland Maya civilization was the product of over a thousand years of cultural evolution in the tropical lowlands of the southern half of the Yucatan peninsula, largely in what is now the Peten district of Guatemala. By the end of the eighth century A.D., the lowland Maya had achieved an impressive degree of intellectual, social, and artistic development. Their economic, religious, and social structures were highly evolved. Their writing system was the most sophisticated in the New World. They had made important discoveries in mathematics and astronomy. And their architecture, pottery, and painting remain to be aesthetically impressive. At least twenty major centers and scores of smaller centers flourished in and adjacent to the Peten. Then suddenly their civilization began its rapid decline.

The decline can be dated fairly precisely because the Maya were enthusiastic monument builders and invariably inscribed calendrical information on their monuments. In the more important centers stelae were placed periodically in the stucco floors of plazas, usually facing important temples. In A.D. 790 nineteen of the major centers erected stelae. In A.D. 889, a year when tradition dictated that stelae be erected, only three centers erected stelae. Other monumental construction halted just as abruptly. The last known Classic Period calendrical inscription of any sort was carved in A.D. 909.

Archaeologists believe that within a period of fifty to one hundred years many of the centers and their immediate surroundings were completely abandoned and in most of the others there was only desultory occupancy. The area was never significantly populated again. According to one archaeologist, what have "intrigued scholars and produced the debates on the topic of the Southern Maya decline are the suddenness of the collapse and, more importantly, the fact that it was correlated with a massive population loss over an enormous area."[2]

Traditional accounts of the collapse tend to stress a single explanatory fact: natural catastrophe, ecological failure, internal revolt, external invasion, and so on. More recent explanations invariably combine elements of several of the traditional explanations. Archaeologists naturally disagree about how to explain the collapse. But they also disagree about what constitutes "the collapse."

Disagreement about what needs to be explained is typical of explanatory disagreement in historical studies. While it is not an extra source of philosophical problems, it can greatly complicate an exposition of how historians argue that one explanation is better than its competitors. To simplify, I shall ignore for the time being disagreement over what constitutes "the collapse" and assume that there is some sentence, or conjunction of sentences, which all archaeologists would agree adequately characterizes what it is they are trying to explain. When I refer to *the collapse* I intend to refer to the fact which this sentence, or conjunction of sentences, asserts to be the case. Later on, I shall explain why this simplifying assumption is innocuous.

My first task is to sketch briefly the main arguments archaeologists have used for and against a representative sample of explanations of the collapse. I shall number these arguments to facilitate cross-reference later. After this survey, I shall suggest a taxonomy of these arguments, and then use this taxonomy to address the larger issue of how archaeologists of the collapse have tried to show that their explanations are better than competing explanations. Finally, I shall consider how my account of the debate over the collapse relates to the larger question of how historians generally defend their explanations.

Catastrophe explanations explain the collapse by postulating natural disasters: earthquakes, hurricanes, climactic changes, epidemics, and so on. The *earthquake explanation*, for instance, postulates that there were severe earthquakes in the southern lowlands in the Late Classic, and that these earthquakes explain the collapse. The evidence adduced for this explanation consists of (1.1) certain aspects of the present ruined condition of Classic centers, and (1.2) the fact that in modern times severe earthquakes are common in the highlands immediately south of Peten.[3]

The earthquake explanation has been criticized on two major grounds. The first is that there is little evidence that there were serious earthquakes in the lowlands in the Late Classic. Most critics concede that relevant aspects of the present ruined conditions of the centers could be a consequence of earthquakes, but they insist (1.3) that they could as likely be a consequence of other causes as well. According to Adams, "it is very difficult to detect the difference between earthquake damage, structural failure and deterioration after abandonment."[4] The second criticism is that severe earthquakes, even if they did take place, are not a sufficient explanation of the collapse. The evidence in support of this criticism is (1.4) that no comparable region is known to have been permanently abandoned as a consequence of earthquakes, and (1.5) that earthquakes are not now and, so far as is known, were not in Classic times as severe in the lowlands as in the adjacent highlands where indigenous societies have survived serious earthquakes down to the present day.[5]

Ecology explanations, while varying greatly in details, tend to attribute the collapse to environmental deterioration caused by overpopulation and overly intensive agriculture, the latter leading to loss of soil fertility, excessive growth of grasses (savannaization), or soil erosion. The *subsistence failure expla-*

nation, for instance, postulates two facts to explain the collapse: a significant growth in population among the Maya during the Late Classic; and almost exclusive dependence of the Maya for their food on forest swidden maize agriculture.[6] According to this explanation, as Maya population increased, the swidden cycle had to be shortened, thus robbing the soil of valuable nutrients and lessening the yield of each planting. With shortened cycles the forest did not develop sufficiently to choke out weed growth. Weeds had to be removed by hand, rather than burned, a nearly impossible task for the Maya given the difficulties of hand weeding and the large areas of land under cultivation. Eventually, shortened cycles led to the development of grassy savannas which replaced much of the forest. When this happened, the land was virtually lost as cropland since the Maya had no plow to turn the soil.

Three considerations are said to support the claim that the Maya were almost exclusively dependent upon forest swidden maize agriculture for their food: (2.01) modern lowland Maya have a quasi-religious allegiance to forest swidden maize agriculture; (2.02) population distribution patterns in and around Maya centers were compatible with what one would expect under a system of forest swidden agriculture; and (2.03) such a system was the most productive one available to the Classic Maya.[7]

Arguments that there was a population boom in the Late Classic are complicated, but depend primarily on (2.04) the discovery of surviving house mounds, low stone platforms upon which the Maya built their houses, and their associated ceramic and refuse deposits.[8]

The claim that these two explanatory facts—dependence on forest swidden maize agriculture, and a population boom—led to a failure of the Maya subsistence system is supported by (2.05) contemporary laboratory studies of soil chemistry and agricultural yield under circumstances presumed to have obtained for the Classic Maya, (2.06) observation of the operation of analogous systems in other parts of the world, and, to a lesser extent, (2.07) indications of malnutrition in Late Classic skeletal remains.[9]

Contemporary critics of the subsistence failure explanation usually concede that there was a Late Classic population boom in the lowlands, that this put a serious strain on the Maya subsistence system, and that this strain played some part in the collapse. For instance, Sabloff and Willey, in a paper arguing for the likelihood and importance of external invasion as a partial explanation of the collapse, concede that

> it seems highly probable that the balance between agricultural man and nature in the Southern Maya Lowlands was a precarious one, one that the strain of overpopulation—for which there is good evidence in Late Classic Period times—might have seriously disturbed and one that an historical event, such as invasion by an external enemy, might well have upset.[10]

Thus, the major contemporary critics of the subsistence failure explanation do not question the fact of subsistence strain, but instead question the explanatory importance assigned to this fact. Some of these criticisms merely question that subsistence strain is a sufficient explanation of the collapse. These employ a familiar strategy: (2.08) areas are mentioned which were subject to population problems as serious as, and an ecology no more favorable than, that in the Peten, but which nevertheless did not collapse.[11] Other criticisms go beyond questioning the sufficiency of subsistence strain and attempt further to minimize its importance relative to other explanatory facts. These criticisms usually question either the extent to which the Maya depended on forest swidden maize agriculture or the extent to which this dependence had deleterious effects.

Critics have questioned the extent to which the Maya depended on forest swidden agriculture by arguing (2.09) that the Maya cultivated root crops and ramon (bread nut) in addition to maize. Sanders, for instance, argues that "recent surveys by the Tikal Project have demonstrated an extraordinarily close relationship between the densities of ramon and housesites that indicates beyond any reasonable doubt that the Maya did plant groves of ramon trees near their houses."[12] Critics have also argued (2.10) that the Maya may have farmed their swamplands in addition to the forest,

(2.11) that forest swidden agriculture was probably supplemented by the less efficient grass swidden system, and (2.12)
that the Maya probably imported some foodstuffs.[13]

Some critics doubt that forest swidden agriculture seriously
diminished the maize crop. While conceding that a shortened
swidden cycle would result in less yield per labor hour, these
critics claim (2.13) that with an abundant labor supply a shortened cycle may nevertheless have resulted in a greater net
yield of maize.[14] Many also question whether a shortened
cycle in the Peten led to the development of savannas. They
note (2.14) the absence of centers from present savanna areas
and the fact that (2.15) modern grassy roads and town plazas
in the Peten, even ones that have been established for many
years, quickly revert to forest if unattended.

Finally, some critics mention (2.16) that Copan and Quiri-
qua, to the southeast of the Peten, were two of the earliest
centers to cease building even though they were situated in
areas so fertile and so well watered that exhaustion of their
agricultural resources seems highly unlikely.[15]

Social explanations attribute the collapse to some sort of social dysfunction. Peasant revolt, intracenter warfare, external
invasion, trade disruption, and even an unfavorable sex ratio
have been proposed as explanations of the collapse. J.E.S.
Thompson's *peasant revolt explanation* postulates that the peasant class deposed, and probably destroyed, the elite class, thus
putting an end to elite class activities, such as monument
building, but that the peasants remained to populate the centers.[16] In other words, Thompson argues that the Maya suffered a decline of civilization without a corresponding decline
of population.

Thompson's main evidence that there was a peasant revolt
is (3.1) certain damage to and alteration of monuments,
which he argues are best explained as deliberate acts of vandalism against the elite class. But Thompson also argues for
an interpretation of Mayan sociopolitical structure according
to which (3.2) there was economic and ideological motivation
for peasant revolt and (3.3) the elite class lacked those powers
of coercion which would have protected it from internal
revolts.

Thompson appeals to two sorts of evidence in defense of his claim for a large, Post-Classic population in the Peten: (3.4) artifacts and burial remains in the centers that, he claims, were deposited after the collapse; (3.5) the fact that "there was a considerable population in the region in the sixteenth century" composed of individuals who, he claims, are most reasonably regarded as "descendants of the original peasant population of the ninth century."[17]

When Thompson first proposed his explanation it was debatable whether the lowland centers were virtually abandoned during the Late Classic. Few archaeologists believe this is still debatable. According to Sanders, "virtually all recent archaeological studies in the southern lowlands agree that there was a catastrophic population loss."[18] According to Culbert, it is "extremely unlikely that anything yet to be discovered will change the conclusion that the Classic Maya of the southern lowlands suffered one of the world's great demographic disasters . . . population loss may well have been in excess of a million people within a single century."[19] Thus, one major criticism of Thompson's explanation is (3.6) that even if there was a peasant revolt, it fails to explain why the centers were depopulated. Many critics also argue that there is not enough evidence that there was a peasant revolt since (3.7) the evidence of vandalism and of the vulnerability of the elite class to internal revolt favors certain competing explanations as much as it favors a peasant revolt explanation.[20]

According to the *invasion explanation*, the collapse is explained by a foreign, probably Mexican, invasion of the southern lowlands in the Late Classic. Scholars disagree as to the identity of the invaders and the timing and locus of the initial invasion. They agree in appealing to two sorts of evidence. First, (4.1) there is physical evidence of a foreign presence at several lowland centers. This consists mostly of ceramic remains which suggest the introduction of foreign pottery traditions, but also includes depictions on several stelae at Seibal of unusual looking people with waist-length hair and bone nose ornaments, both unknown among the lowland Maya. Secondly, (4.2) there is substantial evidence of a Toltec invasion of Yucatan, north of the Peten, prior to or contem-

poraneous with the collapse of the southern lowland civilization. Some invasion theorists argue that "since Yucatan was
obviously invaded at about this time, it would be strange if the
south had been completely untouched."[21]

The invasion explanation has been criticized as insufficient
on the grounds that it does not explain the depopulation
which occurred. Although the invaders might have killed off
the indigenous population, critics argue this is unlikely since
(4.3) the invaders in the Yucatan did not kill off the population there, and, as one invasion theorist concedes, "even remarkably savage invasions, given pre-industrial instruments
of homicide, have not characteristically depopulated entire
regions. . . ."[22]

It is possible that the invaders upset the delicate subsistence
balance, precipitating widespread starvation and/or migration. But critics argue that (4.4) although widespread starvation might account for a decline in population, it does not
explain the almost total depletion which took place.[23] In any
case, such an account tends to reduce invasion to trigger
status and shift the explanatory burden to factors having to
do with the vulnerability of Mayan society.

Migration could have contributed to population loss. But
there is little evidence that widespread migration occurred.
Sanders has suggested a migration into the Guatemalan highlands to the south of the lowlands. His evidence is drawn
from population estimates for the highlands, linguistic differ-
entiation, and archaeological remains. But critics have rejected his suggestion on the grounds that (4.5) if it were true,
there would be more evidence for it in the ceramic remains
than there is.[24] Cowgill has theorized that there were a series
of Mexican invasions, lasting possibly as long as several gen-
erations, which affected the entire lowlands and substantially
reduced the lowlands population, after which the invaders
established a capital at Chichen Itza, to the north of the lowlands, and forced resettlement of the remaining lowlands
population to localities within easy reach of Chichen Itza.[25]
But Cowgill concedes there is little evidence for his theory
and claims only that it is consistent with the evidence which
exists. In sum, most archaeologists feel that invasion without

mass killing and/or substantial migration would have been insufficient for the collapse, and that there is little positive evidence for an invasion accompanied by mass killing and/or substantial migration.

Another difficulty facing the invasion explanation is (4.6) that at many centers, evidence of a foreign presence does not support the claim that there was a foreign presence *before* the collapse. Some critics argue that the foreign presence is as likely a consequence as a cause of the collapse. And some claim (4.7) that at centers such as Tikal it is more likely that the collapse preceded the foreign presence.[26]

How can the data just presented increase our understanding of how historians—in this case, archaeologists—defend the explanations they propose? Two points emerge clearly: these archaeologists argue as if their objective were to show that their favored explanations are better than the best competing explanations; and they defend their favored explanations both by affirmative arguments—by arguing directly for them—and by negative arguments—by arguing directly against competing explanations.

This integrated affirmative and negative argumentative strategy is typical of explanatory justification in historical studies (and also, it is worth noting, of theoretical justification in science and philosophy). For this reason, one can understand how historians actually defend their explanations only by viewing explanatory justification in historical studies as a competitive affair. Any account of explanatory justification in historical studies that focuses on the relationship between evidence and just one explanation at a time, as does, for instance, the positivist account, is bound to be far removed from the dynamics of actual explanatory controversies.

How then can we sort out the seeming chaos of arguments that play a role in the debate over the collapse? To begin, note that each of the explanations just surveyed can be expressed in the form, *that p* (at least partially) explains *that q*, where *p* and *q* are replaced by complete sentences in the indicative mood. For example, *that* there were severe earthquakes in the Peten in late Classic times explains the fact *that* the Lowland

Maya Civilization collapsed in late Classic times. Let us use the term "explanans" to refer to the sentence which replaces p in explanations of this form, the term "explanatory fact" to refer to what the explanans asserts to be the case, the term "explanandum" to refer to the sentence which replaces q, and the term "explanandum event" to refer to what the explanandum asserts to be the case.

With this terminology in hand, the arguments used by archaeologists of the collapse can now be divided into three kinds, depending on whether they are directed at the truth, the explanatory relevance, or the sufficiency of the explanation to which they are addressed directly:

> *Arguments of kind (1)*: Affirmative arguments are intended to increase the likelihood, negative arguments to decrease the likelihood, that a particular explanans (or explanandum) is true;
>
> *Arguments of kind (2)*: Affirmative arguments are intended to increase the likelihood, negative arguments to decrease the likelihood, that a particular explanans is at least a partial explanation of its explanandum;
>
> *Arguments of kind (3)*: Affirmative arguments are intended to increase the likelihood, negative arguments to decrease the likelihood, that a particular explanans is a sufficient explanation of its explanandum.

So, for instance, an affirmative argument of kind (2) is intended to increase the likelihood that the explanans of a favored explanation explains its explanandum, and such an argument does this by arguing directly for the explanatory relevance of the explanans to the explanandum. A negative argument of kind (3) is intended to diminish the likelihood that the explanans of a non-favored, competing explanation is a sufficient explanation of its explanandum, and it does this by arguing directly against its being sufficient. And so on.[27]

Within the framework provided by this taxonomy of the arguments, it is possible to explain rather simply how arguments of each of these kinds actually works. Consider, first, affirmative arguments of kind (1), that is, arguments that the explanans of a favored explanation is true. Such arguments are almost always attempts to show that certain data are best explained by facts the existence of which increases the likelihood that the explanans of a favored explanation is true.[28] Usually this strategy consists of attempts to show that certain data are best explained by the explanatory facts postulated by the favored explanation. Examples include the attempt to show that certain aspects of the present ruined Classic centers are best explained by the fact that there were severe earthquakes in the Peten in the Late Classic, and the attempt to show that certain damage to monuments is best explained by the fact that there was a peasant revolt of such and such a kind in the Late Classic.[29] However, sometimes this strategy consists of attempts to show that certain data are best explained by facts which differ from, but increase the likelihood of, the explanatory facts postulated by the favored explanation; for example, the best explanation of the prevalence in modern times of severe earthquakes in the highlands immediately south of Peten presumably postulates certain facts concerning relatively permanent aspects of the geology of the area which increase the likelihood that there were severe earthquakes in the Peten in the Late Classic.[30]

Negative arguments of kind (1) attempt to show that there is no evidence for and/or evidence against the explanans of some non-favored competing explanation. The claim that there is no evidence for an explanans is simply the claim that there is no good affirmative argument of kind (1) for that explanans, for example, that there are no data which are better explained by the earthquake explanation than by some competing explanation.[31] The argument that there is evidence against an explanans takes one of two closely related forms. The first mentions certain data that do not exist but would likely exist if the explanans were true; for example, the claim that there was a severe epidemic in the Late Classic has been criticized on the grounds that there is neither evidence of Late Classic mass burials nor traces of epidemic diseases in the recovered skeletal material.[32] The second mentions certain data that exist but likely would not exist if the explanans were true. For example, the claim that the Maya were almost exclusively dependent for their food upon forest swidden maize agriculture has been criticized on the grounds that

there is a close relationship between ramon trees and house
sites which is best explained by supposing that the Maya
planted ramon trees near their houses.[33]

Earlier I made the simplifying assumption that archaeologists agree about what constitutes the collapse, and I promised to explain later why this assumption is innocuous. Now
I can explain. The reason is that the strategies historians
employ to determine whether an explanans is true are exactly
the same as those they employ to determine whether an explanandum is true. In describing affirmative and negative
arguments of kind (1), I have explained what those strategies
are, at least in so far as they show up in the debate over the
collapse. It would be redundant also to survey the strategies
historians employ to argue that an explanandum is true.[34]

Affirmative arguments of kind (2), that is, arguments that
an explanans at least partially explains its explanandum, are
designed to show that facts of the same sort as at least some
of the facts mentioned in the explanans have a lawful relationship to facts of the same sort as at least some of the explanandum events. In the debate over the Maya collapse, such
arguments were rarely given; it was simply assumed that the
explanans, if true, explains the explanandum. When such
arguments were given, it was either because the relevance of
the explanatory facts to the explanandum event was not of a
familiar sort, or, though familiar, its applicability to the case
at hand had been challenged.

When affirmative arguments of kind (2) were given, they
were either claimed positive correlations between other instances of facts of the relevant kinds or appeals to theoretical
considerations, or both. An example of the former is Sander's
claim, in support of the subsistence failure explanation, that
recent evidence "from Africa and Indonesia very strongly
supports the position that there is an overall succession from
forest to grass when population densities reach certain levels
in swidden agriculture."[35] Since Sanders does not think agricultural strain was sufficient for the collapse, he intends his
argument to support only that the growth of savannas and
the consequent agricultural strain partially explain the collapse. And Shimkin has argued on the basis of both compara-

tive and theoretical evidence, the latter simply an application of medical science, that archaeologists have underestimated the destructive effect on the Maya of epidemic and endemic diseases.[36]

In the debate over the collapse, I found a few arguments clearly intended to be affirmative arguments of kind (2), but none clearly intended to be affirmative arguments of kind (3). No one claimed to be showing that some explanans was a sufficient explanation of the collapse or of any other explanandum. On the other hand, negative arguments of kind (3) were quite common, whereas negative arguments of kind (2) were almost nonexistent.[37] This is just what one would expect of cautious archaeologists. Since it is much easier to show that an explanans is a partial, rather than a sufficient, explanation of its explanandum, on those rare occasions when an argument for explanatory relevance is required, only an argument for partial relevance is attempted. And since it is much easier to show that some competing explanation is not sufficient than it is to show that it is not even partial, that is all that is usually attempted.

It may seem curious that while affirmative arguments of kind (3) were nonexistent, negative arguments of kind (3) were common. If no one claimed to have provided a sufficient explanation, why are archaeologists so intent on showing that explanations that had been provided are not sufficient? The answer is that negative arguments of kind (3) are a common part of an argumentative strategy which is designed to show that a given explanans partially explains some explanandum. The main role of negative arguments of kind (3) is to "make room" for an extra explanatory fact. Imagine, for instance, that you thought extant explanations of some event were incomplete in that they didn't mention some explanatory fact which you thought should be mentioned. How could you show that mention of this explanatory fact should be included? An obvious strategy is to show via negative arguments of kind (3) that explanations which do not mention this explanatory fact are not sufficient, thereby establishing that mention of *some* explanatory fact must be added to those explanations, and hence strengthening the case that mention of the explanatory fact which you favor should be added. This is why negative arguments of kind (3) are so common. And it is one of two reasons—I shall explain the other in the Appendix—why negative arguments of kind (3) are of more than usual philosophical interest.

Affirmative arguments of kind (3), arguments that some favored explanans is sufficient, and negative arguments of kind (2), arguments that some non-favored explanans is causally irrelevant, played no important role in the debate over the collapse. I shall not discuss them further except to note once again that the absence of affirmative arguments of kind (3) in this debate and in most other historical debates is part of the reason why accounts of the justification of historical explanation which focus primarily on what it takes to show that an explanation is sufficient rarely shed much light on explanatory controversy in historical studies.

Negative arguments of kind (3), arguments that some non-favored, competing explanation is not sufficient, took three different forms. One form was designed to show that although facts of the same sorts as the explanatory facts often occur, they have never been known to bring about events of the same sort as the explanandum event. For example, explanations which postulate earthquakes or hurricanes to explain the collapse are criticized as insufficient on the grounds that although earthquakes and hurricanes are quite common, their known effects have always been local and sporadic, never the decimation of an entire civilization.[38] Thus, although earthquakes or hurricanes may have played a role in the collapse, it is unlikely they were sufficient.

A second variety of negative argument of kind (3) is the claim that an explanation does not explain the difference between the situation in which the explanandum event occurred and some specific comparison. For example, Andrews questioned the sufficiency of the subsistence failure explanation on the grounds that although the Rio Bec area probably had an ecology which was virtually identical to that of the Northern Peten, only fifty miles to the south, "the dense populations of the Rio Bec continued successfully for a number of centuries after the Northern Peten centers were largely abandoned."[39]

Finally, the sufficiency of an explanation is often questioned on theoretical grounds. For instance, laboratory studies on soil depletion are sometimes cited as evidence that the
forest swidden system of agriculture practiced by the Maya
was not as hard on the soil as some have claimed. Furthermore, nutritional disease has been rejected as sufficient for
the collapse because "the effect would [have been] a reduction of population to the point where a viable subsistence
system would become reestablished. . . ."[40]

How then did archaeologists of the collapse attempt to show
that one explanation is better than competing explanations?
More generally, how do historians typically attempt to show
this?

Let us begin by assuming, for the sake of simplification,
that only two factors are relevant in determining which of two
competing explanations is better: the degree to which each is
justified by the available evidence, and the degree to which
each is sufficient. On this assumption, the larger question of
how historians show that one explanation of some event is
better than competing explanations of that event reduces to
three simpler questions:

Q1: How do historians show that one explanation is better
    justified than competing explanations?
Q2: How do historians show that one explanation is more nearly
    sufficient than competing explanations?
Q3: What is the relationship between showing that one explana-
    tion is better justified and/or more nearly sufficient than
    competing explanations and showing that it is better than
    competing explanations?

Answers to these questions are suggested by our survey of
the debate over the collapse. I shall first explain what these
answers are, and then return to the simplifying assumption
which allowed us to reduce the larger question to the three
simpler questions.

A1: Archaeologists showed that one explanation of the collapse is better justified than competing explanations primarily by a combination of affirmative arguments of kind (1),
which support the truth of the explanans of the favored ex-

planation, and negative arguments of kinds (1) and (3), which question both the truth and the sufficiency of the explanantia of competing explanations.

The vast majority of affirmative arguments for the justification of an explanation consist of data claimed to be best explained by the explanans of that explanation. Negative arguments which question the truth of the explanantia of nonfavored competing explanations usually correct data put forth as evidence for such explanantia and/or suggest alternative more congenial ways in which such data might be explained. Negative arguments which question the sufficiency of non-favored competing explanations almost always use one or another of the three strategies specified above in the discussion of negative arguments of kind (3).

A2: Archaeologists showed that one explanation of the collapse is more nearly sufficient than competing explanations almost exclusively by arguing via negative arguments of kind (3) that non-favored competing explanations are not sufficient, and then by supplementing the explanans of the best justified partial explanations of the collapse. They did the latter by adding to the explanatory facts of these partial explanations additional explanatory facts which they felt were the best justified addenda available. For example, although most contemporary archaeologists of the collapse subscribe to some version of the subsistence failure explanation, they recognize that it does not account adequately for the depopulation that occurred. Thus, they add to the subsistence failure explanation an addendum to account for the depopulation. For example, Sanders argues that the explanans of his version of the subsistence failure explanation should be supplemented with information postulating a migration from the southern lowlands to the highlands south of Peten.[41] Sanders does not present much evidence for his addendum. But he feels the need for an addendum, and argues that his addendum is better justified than the most plausible competing addenda.

The kinds of arguments which are used in the debate over the collapse to support the claim that one explanation is more nearly sufficient than competing explanations are quite similar to the kinds used to support the claim that one explanation is better justified than competing explanations. In both cases, they are mainly arguments supportive of the explanans, or of an addendum to the explanans, of a favored explanation and arguments critical of the truth or sufficiency of the explanantia of competing explanations.

A3: The notion of one explanation being *better justified* than another or *more nearly sufficient* than another is clearer than the notion of one explanation being simply *better* than another. The reason is that we do not know what collectively determines which of two competing explanations is better. I shall explain below one important reason why we do not know.

The answer to Q3 is that, *all else being equal*, an explanation that is better justified than another or more nearly sufficient than another is better, but an explanation that is better justified but less nearly sufficient is neither better nor worse than one that is less well justified but more nearly sufficient. Thus, archaeologists deciding whether to advocate a particular explanation of the collapse weigh the advantages of superior justification against the advantages of greater approximation to sufficiency. Sometimes, if an explanation is known to be insufficient, an archaeologist will advocate a more nearly sufficient but less well justified explanation which includes the former. Sometimes an archaeologist might prefer to advocate a better justified, but less nearly sufficient explanation. Within rather broad limits such differences among archaeologists simply reflect temperamental differences—whether one is cautious or daring—rather than allegiance to some systematic method for making such decisions.

I have described how archaeologists have argued that some favored explanation of the collapse is better justified and/or more nearly sufficient than non-favored competing explanations, and I have used that description as a basis for suggesting a partial answer to the question of how historians show that one explanation is better than competing explanations. I believe, but have not shown, that the sorts of arguments and argumentative strategies that archaeologists of the collapse have employed are used quite generally in historical studies. If they are, then the discussion above should help us to understand two important reasons why positivist accounts of the justification of historical explanation so often look like a distorted caricature of actual historical practice. First, such accounts typically underestimate the importance of justifying the explanans and overestimate the importance of justifying covering generalizations. The explanantia of those explanations which are the foci of most explanatory controversies in historical studies are almost always subjected to vigorous criticism; that such explanantia at least partially explain their explananda, given that both explanantia and explananda are true, is a much less frequent topic of debate. Secondly, positivist accounts typically all but ignore the comparative evaluation of competing explanations, or, if they do consider it, they focus mainly on affirmative arguments and consider them through the lens of the positivist theory. It is characteristic of explanatory controversy in historical studies that one argues for a favored explanation not only via affirmative arguments but also via negative arguments which reduce the plausibility of competing explanations.

I have made some simplifying assumptions. The most important of these is that I have assumed that there are only two relevant factors in determining which of two competing explanations are better, the degree to which each is justified by the available evidence and the degree to which each is sufficient. This assumption works pretty well for the purpose of analyzing the debate over the collapse because the structure of that debate is relatively simple. More full-blooded historical debates, for instance, the debate over the causes of the English Civil War, are invariably more complex in ways which undermine this assumption. The most important of these ways is that explanations do not compete with each other on their own, but rather as part of larger historical interpretations.

In other words, in full-blooded historical debates, while individual explanations compete with each other, the interpretations of which they are a part, also explanatory structures, compete with each other too, and the outcome of the

competition among individual explanations is often profoundly affected by the outcome of this larger interpretational competition, and vice versa. Hence, an adequate account of the ways historians justify individual explanations
must explain the relationship between explanatory competition and interpretational competition, that is, it must not only
be *comparative* in the ways I have illustrated, it must also be
holistic. Thus, an adequate account must be about as far removed from a non-comparative approach as one can get.[42]
The complications engendered by the interdependence of
explanation and interpretation is one important reason why
we do not know what collectively determines which of two
competing explanations is better.

This holistic aspect of explanatory competition shows up in
the debate over the collapse primarily in connection with
J.E.S. Thompson's peasant revolt explanation. Thompson's
claim that certain damage to and alteration of Mayan monuments are best explained as acts of deliberate vandalism
against the elite class both supports and depends upon his
overall interpretation of Mayan sociopolitical structure. But
perhaps the clearest way to illustrate this holistic aspect of
explanatory controversy is to digress briefly from the debate
over the collapse and consider a different example.

On December 23, 1888, Vincent Van Gogh, then thirty-five
years old, cut off the lower half of his left ear. He took it to
a brothel and gave the half-ear to a prostitute named Rachel,
requesting that she "keep this object carefully."[43]

Why did Van Gogh cut off his ear and then give it to
Rachel? Many explanations have been proposed, a few of
which may be summarized as follows:

1. Van Gogh was frustrated by his beloved brother Theo's recent
   engagement to be married and by his own failure to establish
   a satisfactory working and living relationship with Paul Gaugin. These frustrations led Van Gogh to behave aggressively,
   first toward Gaugin, and then, when that failed, toward himself.
2. Van Gogh was troubled by homosexual impulses aroused by
   the presence of Gaugin. His response to this arousal was to cut
   off his ear, a symbolic self-castration.

3. In the months preceding Van Gogh's self-mutilation there were several articles in the local newspaper reporting the exploits of Jack the Ripper. The articles described how Jack physically mutilated prostitutes, sometimes cutting off their ears. The reports gave rise to emulators. Van Gogh was one of these emulators. Since Van Gogh was a masochist rather than a sadist, he reversed Jack's act by mutilating himself and bringing his ear to a prostitute.

4. Van Gogh was deeply impressed by bullfights he had seen in Arles in which the victorious matador was given the ear of the vanquished bull, displayed it to the crowd, and then gave it to the lady of his choice. Van Gogh, in cutting off his own ear and giving it to Rachel, was emulating this ritual.

5. Van Gogh identified with prostitutes. A few months before his self-mutilation, he wrote, "The whore is like meat in a butcher shop." In cutting off his ear, he assumed the role of both customer and prostitute, treating his own body like meat in a butcher shop, thereby expressing his identification with prostitutes.

Which, if any, of these explanations is best? Because of the kinds of explanations they are, how we answer will depend not just on evidence locally relevant to Van Gogh's act of self-mutilation, but also on a larger interpretive analysis. In order to evaluate competing explanations of the ear-cutting incident, we have to know first what Van Gogh was capable of doing, and for what sorts of reasons. To know that, we need an interpretation of Van Gogh's history and personality in order to assess what sort of a person he was at the time he cut off his ear. For instance, the first explanation listed above has been supported by appeal to oedipal considerations. Gaugin is said to have represented Van Gogh's hated father, and Van Gogh's aggression toward Gaugin, his subsequent self-mutilation, and his behavior at the brothel are all said to be symbolic expressions of this hatred. This explanation may or may not be fanciful, but it nicely illustrates the interdependence between the issues of how we should interpret Van Gogh, the man, and how we can best explain why he cut off his ear and gave it to Rachel. Much of the evidence for and against the larger interpretation is relevant to how we explain the ear-cutting incident, and vice versa. In other words, the competition is not just among competing explanations of the incident itself, but also among the larger interpretations in which these local explanations are embedded. The same point could be made if we leave biography and go to political or social history. Ironically, the point is all but made by Murray Murphey in his interesting analysis of alternative interpretations of Bacon's Rebellion, a revolt in Virginia in 1676 that the historian T. J. Wertenbaker interpreted as a prefiguration of the American Revolution. Stressing the interdependence of "fact and interpretation," Murphey notes that how a historian explains Bacon's Laws, passed by the House of Burgesses in June of 1676, depends importantly on his larger interpretational framework, and vice versa. For instance,

> Wertenbaker regarded the rebellion as a conflict between two parties, one representing democracy and the other, autocracy. The June assembly represents the triumph of the democratic faction, and Bacon's Laws the success of this group in enacting its program.[44]

Murphey emphasizes that Wertenbaker's explanation of Bacon's laws depends on assumptions about the parties in the revolt and about the composition of the June assembly which are themselves supported by evidence furnished by the laws. But unfortunately, when Murphey then explains how historians *ought* to defend their explanations, he ignores the inescapable interdependence of explanation and interpretation.

A second important way in which my account of explanatory competition is simplified is that I have assumed that the notion of "competing explanation" is clear enough for us to be able to identify pairs of explanations which are competing explanations. In the debate over the collapse, this is relatively easy to do, but it is not as easy to do for some other debates. Consider, for instance, the alternative explanations listed in the Van Gogh example. Are they all competing explanations, or are some compatible with others?[45] It depends partly on what is meant by "competing explanation." My guess is that "competing explanation" is an epistemic notion: two explanations of an event are competing explanations of that event *if* it is more likely, on the available evidence, that one or the other explains that event than that both explain it.[46] For present purposes, I will not pursue the analysis of "competing explanation" further.

Finally, the debate over the collapse suggests an overly simplified picture of historical dispute in that disagreement over causal importance plays a relatively minor role in that debate. In richer and more mature historical debates, disagreement over causal importance generally plays a central role. For this reason, I shall devote the entire next chapter to the issue of relative causal importance.

The important point for now is that if we are ever to answer the question of how historians show that one explanation is better than competing explanations, that is, if we are ever to know how historians defend the explanations they propose—which in the case of the best, available historical work is probably close to how historians ought to defend the explanations they propose—we shall have to find out by means of detailed case studies of a number of explanatory controversies in historical studies and careful generalization on the basis of these case studies. In the philosophy of history literature, there are few such case studies, despite intense interest over the last forty years in the question of historical explanation. That says something about the philosophy of history, I think—that so far as accounts of explanation are concerned, philosophy of history has been on the wrong track.

The present chapter constitutes only one case study of explanatory competition, and a highly simplified one at that. It is a beginning, but it is not an adequate basis for answering the question of how historians show that one explanation is better than competing explanations. I hope, though, that it at least provides a useful illustration of how we can investigate that question by means of the empirical approach.

Chapter 4

CAUSAL WEIGHTING

Accord to E. H. Carr, "Every historical argument revolves around the question of the priority of causes."[1] Carr's remark is an overstatement, but not by much. Judgments that assign relative importance to causes—henceforth called "weighted explanations"—are at the center of historical controversy. And ambiguities about what they mean and how they should be defended are often major obstacles to the resolution of historical disagreement.

It might seem, then, that the problem of clarifying weighted explanations and of explaining how they should be defended must be a high priority among methodologically-minded historians. It has not been. Although many historians are aware of the importance of the problem, few have devoted much energy to solving it. J. H. Hexter's remarks are unusually candid:

> At one time or another all historians encounter the acute difficulty created by the problem of importance. Particularly with respect to accounting for a particular happening . . . how do we decide that one cluster of antecedents is more or less important than others . . . ? Although we all encounter the problem of importance, we almost never face it. . . . The matter of historical importance is a fair field full of inexplicit and unconscious assumptions. When a historian does have the courage to face the issue of importance, the result is often a quiet desperation, tactfully concealed from the public in the interest of avoiding intellectual scandal.[2]

To make matters worse, many historians seem content to dispatch the problem of causal importance simply by claiming that weighted explanations are subjective. J. Barzun and

53

H. F. Graff, for instance, in the third edition of their highly regarded *The Modern Researcher*, report with approval Edward Lucas White's remark that "if . . . it took malaria-bearing mosquitoes and the spread of Christianity to undo the Roman Empire, then mosquitoes were as necessary as the Christians and neither is paramount to the other."[3] Lawrence Stone, in *The Causes of the English Revolution*, remarks that "in the last resort the imposition of a rank order of relative importance depends not on objective and testable criteria, but on the judgment, sensibility or bias of the historian."[4]

Even among scholars who believe that weighted explanations have an objective meaning, there is some tendency to claim that historians are so incapable of adequately defending weighted explanations that their commitment to them is little more than subjective preference. Ernest Nagel, for instance, after arguing impressively that weighted explanations often have "an undeniably clear and verifiable content," stresses that "it is doubtful in most cases" whether they are "supported by competent evidence" and concludes that historians "are therefore compelled, willy-nilly, to rely on guesses and vague impressions in assigning weights to causal factors."[5]

We need to distinguish two questions: Do weighted explanations mean something objective? And, if they do, can they be defended objectively, so that a historian's preference for one rather than another is not subjective? My answer to both questions is yes. But my main objective is not to answer these two questions, but rather to motivate a shift in philosophical focus from these questions to the question, "How do historians attempt to show that one weighted explanation is better than competing weighted explanations," and then to the question, "How should they attempt to show this?" Since the overriding explanatory objective of historians is to show that their explanations are better than competing explanations, until we understand how they attempt to show that their weighted explanations are better, we shall not understand the logic of explanatory controversy in historical studies. And until we understand that, we shall not be in a position to make realistic methodological recomendations.

The claim, often made, that weighted explanations are subjective raises more questions than it answers. It does not reveal the sense of "subjective" in which they are subjective, or to what degree they are subjective, or whether it is what they mean or how they are defended which makes them subjective, or whether there may be ways to make them less subjective, and so on. And if all weighted explanations are subjective, it should be a serious question whether historians should continue to assert them. Yet few who claim that weighted explanations are subjective advocate that historians abandon them, and those few who do are all but universally ignored.

It is difficult to believe that *all* weighted explanations *mean* something that is normative, or non-factual, or just "a matter of taste." Indeed, weighted explanations that assign relative importance to the causes of *types* of results often appear to be factual. The judgment, say, that driver negligence was more important than mechanical failure as a cause of automobile accidents at a certain place and time seems to be objective. So also do many weighted explanations that assign relative importance to the causes of *particular* results, such as the judgment that Lenin's participation in the Russian October Revolution was a more important cause of its success than was Stalin's participation, or the judgment that Germany's declaration of unrestricted submarine warfare was a more important cause of the United States entry into World War I than was the disclosure of the Zimmermann Note. Historians do not merely assert such weighted explanations, they support them with factual evidence. Whether these explanations are true does not seem to be a normative question or a matter of taste.

Those weighted explanations that are most central to historical studies—also the ones that are most puzzling—assign relative importance to the causes of *particular* results. They are of a sort, for lack of an appropriate theory or an adequate data base, to which formal statistical techniques for assigning weights to causes are not applicable. It is this sort of weighted explanation, if any, that can be most plausibly regarded as subjective. So, if even this sort of weighted explanation can be objective, there is little to be said for the inherent subjectivity of weighted explanations. Henceforth, when I use the term "weighted explanation," I shall mean an explanation of this sort.

William Dray has provided the most interesting argument that weighted explanations *mean* something subjective.[6] He argues convincingly through a careful examination of alternative interpretations of the American Civil War, and more recently through an examination of the dispute between A.J.P. Taylor and his critics over the origins of the Second World War, that historians often use weighted explanations and related causal language in a covertly moral, or at least normative, sense. Dray shows that when historians do this—especially when they do it without recognizing that they are doing it or how they are doing it—they create major obstacles to the resolution of historical disagreements.

Dray argues for these conclusions by showing that historians often attempt to support weighted explanations and attack rival explanations by appeal to considerations such as whether a given course of action was "reasonable" or "moral." For instance, historians who wrote in the immediate wake of the American Civil War tended to divide along sectional lines and to subscribe to what Dray calls "the conspiracy theory." To Southern historians, the fact that the secession of the south (even the firing on Sumter) was a warranted response to a Northern threat was a reason for not regarding it as the cause of the war. To Northern historians, the fact that the South had no constitutional right to secede or any legal claim to federal property was a reason for regarding Southern resistance to rightful occupation as the cause of the war.

One could, of course, disallow such appeals to normative considerations on the grounds that they are irrelevant. But an analysis of what a judgment means is both unjustified and useless unless it reflects the characteristic kinds of evidence that count for and against that kind of judgment. Dray shows that appeals to normative considerations are often regarded by historians as appeals to relevant evidence. But if we admit such appeals as relevant evidence, then we must also concede that the weighted explanations they support are themselves normative.

Dray's argument that historians often appeal to normative considerations to confirm or disconfirm causal explanations illustrates nicely the empirical approach to understanding historical explanation. It also convincingly demonstrates the need for significant methodological reform in historical studies and gives this reform some direction. Surprisingly, Dray rejects the idea that his examination of historical practice demonstrates the need for methodological reform. For instance, in reply to A.J.P. Taylor's claim that "it is not part of the historian's duty to say what ought to have been done, his sole duty is to find out what was done and why," Dray argues that the historian who finds out "what was done and why" must distinguish causes from mere conditions, and the historian who distinguishes causes from conditions cannot help but make moral, or at least normative, judgments.[7] But, in arguing this case, as we shall see in the next chapter, Dray argues fallaciously from factual premises to a conceptual conclusion, or from the claim that historians typically do mean something subjective by their weighted explanations to the conclusion that therefore they must.

A more subtle problem with Dray's argument is that he conflates the distinction, on the one hand, between causes and conditions, and, on the other, between more and less important causes. In other words, he treats judgments that one explanatory fact *caused* or was *the cause of* some result and judgments that one explanatory fact was *more important than another* as a cause of that result as if they were interchangeable. For instance, Dray routinely treats attempts by historians of the American Civil War to assess *the relative importance* of causes as if they were attempts to determine what *caused* the war or some aspect of the war, which he then interprets as attempts to distinguish causes from conditions.[8] Other philosophers also conflate these two distinctions. Morton White, for instance, in his "abnormalist" account of the cause/condition distinction, assumes that "the cause," "the real cause," and "the decisive cause" are often used equivalently and that "more important cause" and "most important cause" imply "the decisive cause."[9] There is no hint in White's account that a further analysis is required for the distinction between more and less important causes in addition to his analysis of the cause/condition distinction.

Historians often encourage this confusion by using causal language carelessly, often conflating the two distinctions. But the important issue is not how historians speak, but whether there are two different sorts of judgments underlying their explanatory practices that must be distinguished in order to understand those practices. I want to argue that there are. Judgments that distinguish causes from conditions and judgments that assign relative importance to causes are not interchangeable. They mean different things and have different functions in historical controversy. They require radically different analyses. And because of the central role of weighted explanations in most mature, explanatory controversies in historical studies, a clear, working understanding of the relationship between these two sorts of judgments is essential to a satisfactory sorting of the central issues.

Consider, first, the cause/condition distinction. Suppose that a fire inspector returns from investigating a house fire and reports that the cause was a short circuit in the wiring near the dining room lights. The short circuit, let us suppose, was one of several factors that contributed to the fire. The presence of an adequate supply of oxygen and the proximity of combustible material also contributed. No doubt other factors contributed as well. The fire inspector chose one of these—the short circuit—and elevated it to the status of "the cause" while ignoring other causally relevant factors, relegating them to the status of "mere conditions." She also, of course, ignored many factors that did not contribute to the fire.

We know why the fire inspector passed over those non-contributory factors. What we want to know is why she passed over all but one of those factors which contributed causally to the fire, elevating only that one to the status of "the cause." We also want to know whether her selection procedure can be understood on the basis of an objective criterion for distinguishing the cause from mere conditions, a criterion applicable not just to this case but across the entire range of cases in which this distinction is made.

A number of philosophers have argued that there is a criterion on the basis of which causes may be distinguished objectively from conditions. These philosophers include C. J. Ducasse, J. Feinberg, S. Gorovitz, H.L.A. Hart, A. Honoré, M. Scriven, R. Shope, and M. White.[10] While their accounts vary greatly in details, there is enough similarity among them to warrant talk of a "consensus account" of the cause/condition distinction. The basic idea of this consensus account is that "the cause" is selected from among contributory causes on the basis of a comparison between the situation in which the result to be explained occurred and some other situation which I shall call "the comparison-situation." In the comparison-situation, events of the same types as the conditions are present, but an event of the same type as the result to be explained is absent. Thus, there must have been some additional factor, "the cause" that was causally relevant to the result to be explained, but that is also an event of a type absent from the comparison-situation.

"The cause," then, like the conditions, contributes to the result, but unlike the conditions, also differentiates between the situation in which the result occurred and the comparison-situation. In the case of the fire inspector's explanation, the comparison-situation might be the house and its immediate environment on all of those prior occasions when the house did not catch fire. On those occasions, oxygen and combustible material were present, but there was no fire. Thus, the short circuit, but not the presence of oxygen or combustible material, differentiates between the situation in which the fire occurred and those prior situations in which there was no fire.

Often, there will be more than one factor that contributes causally to a given result and also differentiates between the situation in which that result occurred and the indicated comparison-situation. When there are several such factors, then they jointly qualify as "the cause," and it is natural to rank them relative to each other in terms of causal importance.

Suppose, for instance, we want to know why Ralph failed his philosophy exam this term even though he got a high mark last term. The following factors, let us suppose, all contributed to his failure this term and also differentiate the situation in which he failed this term from the one in which he got a high mark last term: (1) this term he prepared less for the examination; (2) the examination covered more difficult material; and (3) this term he was powerfully distracted by developments in his personal life. The cause of his failure relative to the indicated comparison-situation will, then, be a conjunction of factors, the ones listed plus any others that might have contributed and differentiate between the two situations. When the cause is a combination of several factors, it is natural to ask whether some were more important than others. Once we learn, for instance, that the three factors listed collectively caused Ralph's failing his philosophy exam, it is natural to ask whether any of these three were more important than the others. In asking this question, we are not asking for another division between causes and conditions, but rather for a different sort of division, one between more and less important causes.

"The cause," then, according to the consensus account, is that contributory cause, or those causes, of the result to be explained that satisfies the following two conditions: (1) it, or they, is not an event of a type present in the comparison-situation; and (2) it, or they, together with events of types that are present in the comparison-situation, is (at least close to) sufficient for the result to be explained. On this account, what should be regarded as "the cause" is relative to a comparison-situation. But it is a purely factual matter whether a factor satisfies requirements (1) and (2) and hence qualifies as "the cause." There is nothing moral or normative about it. In other words, explanations in terms of "the cause" are relative, but not subjective.

There are many possible comparison-situations. The explanatory question that is asked determines which is relevant on a given occasion. In the fire-inspector example, the question might have been, "Why did this house catch fire, when previously it was not on fire?" This question indicates a comparison-situation, and the answer—the short circuit—is a causal condition of the fire that differentiates between the situation in which the fire occurred and this comparison-situation. But different explanatory questions can indicate different comparison-situations and hence elicit different selections of "the cause." Suppose, for instance, that the fire investigation was not of a routine sort but rather part of a special study on the fire potential of short circuits in an experimental housing division where most of the houses were made of a material that is not combustible. Then the question might have been, "Why did this house with a short circuit catch fire, whereas other houses, in the same subdivision also with short circuits, did not catch fire?" This latter question indicates a different comparison-situation, and the answer, or the cause of the fire, will also be different. Presumably, the answer will be that this house was made of a combustible material. To take a more realistic example, compare the question "Why did the Roman Empire in the West succumb in the fifth century to barbarian pressure even though it had successfully resisted barbarian pressure in the previous four centuries?" with the question "Why did the Roman Empire in the West, but not the Roman Empire in the East, succumb in the fifth century to barbarian pressure?" Both questions attempt to elicit "the cause" of the fall of the Roman Empire in the West, but because they indicate different comparison-situations, their correct answers may well differ, and in this case actually do.

Much hinges on whether a clear question that indicates a specific comparison-situation has been asked. But not infrequently in historical studies, answers are given to questions that are either never asked or asked unclearly. Such practices breed confusion. Compare, for instance, either of the latter two historical questions in the preceding paragraph with the question "Why did Rome fall?" The questions in the preceding paragraph indicate specific comparison-situations. The question "Why did Rome fall?" does not. The preceding questions are thus clear in a way the question "Why did Rome fall?" is not.

Sometimes the context in which the historian asks her question or how she answers it allows us to infer which question she is trying to answer, and hence which comparison-situation is applicable to her question. Sometimes not. When we cannot figure out which comparison-situation is intended or appropriate there may be no objective way to evaluate the selection of the cause from among the contributory factors of the result in question. But the important point is that there is a criterion that may be used to distinguish objectively between causes and conditions. On this criterion, a contributory cause qualifies as "the cause" only relative to a particular comparison-situation, and often will not qualify as "the cause" relative to a different comparison-situation; and which comparison-situation is relevant to a causal inquiry is indicated by a properly formulated question that the inquiry is designed to answer. Once a properly formulated question has been asked, it is a purely factual matter how it should be answered.

That the consensus account of the cause/condition distinction is applicable to a great many judgments which distinguish causes from conditions in historical studies is amply defended in the literature from which that account is drawn. There is no need to rehearse that defense here. I believe, contrary to Dray, that the consensus account is correct as an account of how historians usually distinguish causes from conditions. But for present purposes, it does not matter whether I am right about this. What matters is that it is always possible to distinguish causes from conditions on factual grounds by addressing an appropriately formulated explanatory question.[11] Hence, historians are never forced to distinguish causes from conditions on moral or other normative grounds.

If what counts as "the cause" varies with the comparison-situation, and the comparison-situation that is relevant on a given occasion is indicated by a properly formulated explanatory question, what determines which explanatory question should be asked? There is no general answer to this question. It all depends on the purposes to be served by the inquiry in which the question arises. And there is no way to limit these purposes. If our purpose, for instance, is to correct a system that has broken down, as our purpose often is in, say, engineering, economic policy, and medical diagnostic contexts of inquiry, we might ask a question that maximizes our chances of isolating a causal factor that we can manipulate. If our purpose is to assign human responsibility, as it often is in legal and moral contexts of inquiry, we might ask a question that maximizes our chances of isolating a culpable human action. If our purpose is to highlight a cross-cultural comparison, as it often is in comparative historical studies, we might ask a question that maximizes our chances of isolating causal factors that differentiate among the cultures being compared. If our purpose is to construct a narrative account, as it often is in traditional historical studies, we might ask a question that maximizes our chances of isolating a causal factor that differentiates between earlier and later phases of whatever it is whose history we are narrating. And so on.

It may seem, then, that the consensus account does not show that causes may be distinguished objectively from conditions so much as it merely pushes the subjectivity of the selection procedure into the background, for on the consensus account how causes are distinguished from conditions all depends on which question a historian asks, and which question he asks is surely an expression of his values. No doubt a clever sociologist of explanation could show how researchers attempt to control the answers to their empirical inquiries by asking certain causal questions rather than others and hence manipulating the comparison-situations indicated by those questions. So far as I know, there is no such sociological study, although Dray's work is suggestive. But it is important to distinguish between this claim about researcher control and the claim that the cause/condition distinction is subjective. Relativity does not imply subjectivity. And if the case for subjectivity depends on an expression of the inquirer's values through the questions that are asked, rather than how they are answered, then every inquiry, including those in physics, is subjective, but in a rather thin and uninteresting sense of "subjective."

I shall return to the issue of subjectivity in historical studies in the next two chapters. The main point for now is that without first understanding how causes and conditions may be distinguished, it is all but impossible to understand weighted explanations. This is because the distinction be-

tween more and less important causes is typically parasitic on
the distinction between causes and conditions. As in the example of Ralph above, the distinction between more and less
important causes is typically drawn among causes, conditions
having already been excluded from consideration. When historians forget this, as we shall see sometimes happens, they
run into methodological problems. When philosophers do
not notice this, as we have already seen often happens, they
give a distorted account of weighted explanations.

Dray argues that weighted explanations are necessarily
subjective because the distinction between causes and conditions is necessarily subjective. I have shown that his argument
is fallacious by explaining how historians can distinguish between causes and conditions in a factual way. It remains now
to consider whether historians can also make the different
distinction between more and less important causes in a factual way. I shall argue that they can. If my argument is successful, it should answer the subjectivist who argues that
weighted explanations are necessarily subjective because of
what they mean.

But what of subjectivists who argue that even though
weighted explanations may mean something objective, a historian's preference for one weighted explanation over another is usually subjective because historians rarely have adequate evidence to justify such preferences? As we saw in the
last chapter, the problem with this objection is that it is not
true that either the historian has adequate evidence to justify
his explanation in accordance with some non-comparative
standard of justification or else his preference for that explanation is subjective. A historian who has only meager and
ambiguous evidence for a particular weighted explanation
may still be able to show that it is better supported by available
evidence than is any competing weighted explanation. Typically, the most that historians can do to defend any sort of
explanation, weighted or not, is to provide a comparative
justification. But that is enough. There are many explanatory
problems in every branch of inquiry, including the most rig-
orous, where no more than that can be accomplished.

Nothing of methodological importance hinges on whether
historians typically defend their weighted explanations "sub-

jectively," where this is determined by some non-comparative standard of justification. The important issues, for methodological purposes, are, first, how historians typically defend their weighted explanations, and then, whether there is any better way in which they might defend them. Until we can answer these questions we do not understand the logic of explanatory disagreement in historical studies. Once we can answer these questions, we know all that it is practicably useful to know about weighted explanations in historical studies.

What has been done so far in this chapter is to clear the way for illustrating the empirical approach to the investigation of weighted explanations in historical studies. I shall now begin that illustration by considering the grounds one eminent historian gives to support his choice among competing weighted explanations. Then I shall use the data exposed in this investigation to test an analysis of weighted explanations. Finally, I shall use this analysis to help answer the question of how we should choose among competing weighted explanations. In other words, what follows is an illustration of how, by using the empirical approach, one can describe and evaluate the role of weighted explanations in historical studies.

Few problems have attracted more historical talent or sustained more controversy than that of explaining the fall of the Roman Empire in the West. Few have received more meticulous scholarship. More is known today about the circumstances of Rome's fall than ever before, at least in modern times. Yet the controversy over why Rome fell is as vigorous as ever. Many of the difficulties that block further progress are widely recognized: the available evidence is meager and ambiguous; the corpus of useful theory from the social sciences is slender. But other difficulties, some no less serious, are only dimly intimated in the literature on the fall. Of these, one of the most troublesome and ubiquitous, even if rarely acknowledged, is that of determining how one should defend judgments that assign relative degrees of importance to various causes of the fall.

A.H.M. Jones, the late English classicist, is one of the most distinguished twentieth-century historians of the Roman Empire. His views on the fall of the empire in the West are expressed primarily in his major two-volume work, *The Later Roman Empire, 284–602*, published in 1964, and in its shorter sequel, *The Decline of the Ancient World*, published in 1966.[12] In these works, Jones assigns greater causal importance to increased pressure from barbarians, during the fourth and fifth centuries, than to other causes of the fall that he also recognizes. These other causes include a decline in agricultural productivity, depopulation, the expansion and excessive centralization of government, the growth of governmental corruption, the expansion of the army, a crippling tax burden, a growing disequilibrium between economic producers and idle consumers, an increasingly unequal distribution of wealth, civil wars, and a decline in public spirit.

I want to begin by considering first what Jones's reasons are for regarding some causes as more important than others, and then whether they are good reasons. My evaluation of Jones's reasons will be philosophical rather than historical, because I shall not question the truth of any factual claim on which Jones bases his judgments of relative causal importance. I shall assume that these factual claims are true. My objectives are to determine whether these factual claims confirm Jones's weighted explanations, and if so, how.

Jones's argument proceeds on two fronts, both of which involve a comparative perspective. One is a comparison of the circumstances and fates of the Eastern and Western parts of the Empire, the other a comparison of the Western Empire at the time of the fall and the Western Empire during earlier, happier times.

Jones first uses his comparison of the Eastern and Western parts of the Empire to show that increased barbarian pressure on the West was *an* important cause of the fall:

> All the historians who have discussed the decline and fall of the Roman empire . . . tended to forget, or to brush aside, one very important fact, that the Roman empire, though it may have declined, did not fall in the fifth century nor indeed for another thousand years. During the fifth century, while the Western parts were being parceled out into a group of barbarian kingdoms, the empire of the East stood its ground. In the sixth it counterattacked and reconquered Africa from the Vandals and Italy

from the Ostrogoths, and part of Spain from the Visigoths. Before the end of the century, it is true, much of Italy and Spain had succumbed to renewed barbarian attacks, and in the seventh the onslaught of the Arabs robbed the empire of Syria, Egypt, and Africa, and the Slavs overran the Balkans. But in Asia Minor the empire lived on, and later, recovering its strength, reconquered much territory that it had lost in the dark days of the seventh century.

These facts are important, for they *demonstrate* that the empire did not, as some modern historians have suggested, totter into its grave from senile decay, *impelled by a gentle push from the barbarians.*[13]

Let us assume that barbarian pressure was a contributory cause of the fall. What then are Jones's reasons for concluding that barbarian pressure on the West was more than "a gentle push?" The *mere fact* that the East survived while the West collapsed does not show that it was more than a gentle push. If two men were standing on the edge of a cliff, a gentle push to one but not the other may explain radical differences in their respective fates.

Historians often appeal to the fact that one cause, or some set of causes, differentiates between a situation in which the result to be explained occurred and some comparison-situation to conclude that the differentiating cause "caused" or was "the cause" of the result to be explained. Even Jones does this at the end of his discussion of the fall in *The Decline of the Ancient World.* Either ignoring or forgetting his earlier assertion that many causes of the fall were not present, at least to the same degree, in the East, Jones concludes:

It must, however, be emphasized that the eastern empire shared to the full these various weaknesses, economic, social and moral, and that it nevertheless survived for centuries as a great power. It was the increasing pressure of the barbarians, concentrated on the weaker western half of the empire, that caused the collapse.[14]

If increased barbarian pressure on the West "caused" the fall of the West, that shows that it "made the difference" between the situation in which the fall took place and some comparison-situation in which there was no fall. But that is all it shows.

It does not show that increased barbarian pressure on the West was more than "a gentle push" or that it was more important than other contributory causes of the fall, which have been relegated to the status of mere background conditions.

Any special causal status that derives solely from the fact that a contributory cause differentiates between the situation in which a result occurred and some particular comparison-situation holds only relative to that comparison-situation. It is always possible that a different contributory cause differentiates between the situation in which the result occurred and some different comparison-situation. Jones employs more than one comparison in his analysis of the causes of the fall. In addition to the East/West comparison, he compares the Empire in the West during the fourth and fifth centuries, just prior to the fall, with the Empire during the first three centuries A.D. The differentiating causes in the former comparison are not identical to the differentiating causes in the latter comparison. The latter causes include the "worsening" during the fourth and fifth centuries of many internal causes of the fall, as well as the administrative separation of the Eastern and Western parts of the Empire. But, even on the assumption that increased barbarian pressure caused the fall relative to some particular comparison-situation, we cannot conclude that it was more than "a gentle push" nor that it was more important than other contributory causes of the fall, which, relative to that particular comparison-situation, are considered as mere background conditions.

We have seen that Jones can distinguish between cause and condition and how he can do so. What we have not yet seen is how he can get beyond the cause/condition distinction and defend his main weighted explanation, that is, his claim that barbarian pressure on the West is more important than other causes of the fall. Jones has claimed that the Eastern and Western parts of the Empire were not on the edge of a cliff. But the mere fact that the Eastern Empire survived while the Western Empire collapsed does not show that he is right. Perhaps Jones's point is that the manner in which the East survived shows that the East and the West were not on the edge of a cliff. Even if we were to assume this is Jones's point and that he is right that the East and the West were not on the edge of a cliff, Jones still has not shown that barbarian pressure on the West was more than a gentle push.

In addition to greater barbarian pressure on the West than on the East, Jones recognizes other contributory causes of the fall that were not present in the East. Jones argues, for instance, that the West was less populous, less intensely cultivated, poorer, and less politically stable than the East. In other words, the West had various internal weaknesses to a greater degree than the East and was subjected to more pressure from barbarians than was the East. Some independent basis is needed for comparing the relative importance of these two facts. Until this is provided, one cannot dismiss the possibility that these other differentiating internal weaknesses together with causes common to the East and the West were sufficient, or all but sufficient, to cause the fall.[15]

Jones eventually uses his comparison between the circumstances and fates of the Eastern and Western parts of the Empire to make the point that increased pressure from barbarians was "the major cause" of the fall. The passage in which he claims this, from *The Later Roman Empire*, concludes his explanation of the fall and provides a better synopsis of his overall argument than any other single passage in his books.

> The Western government on the other hand was almost bankrupt by the end of Valentinian III's reign and had virtually abandoned conscription, relying almost entirely on barbarian federates. The collapse of the West was however by no means entirely attributable to its internal weaknesses, for the government had by now lost to the barbarians many of the provinces on which it had relied for revenue and recruits, and those which it still controlled had suffered so severely from the ravages of the barbarians that they had to be allowed remission of taxation.
>
> Of the manifold weaknesses of the later Roman empire some, the increasing maldistribution of wealth, the corruption and the extortion of the administration, the lack of public spirit and the general apathy of the population, were to a large extent due to

internal causes. But some of the more serious of these weaknesses were the result, direct or indirect, of barbarian pressure. Above all the need to maintain a vastly increased army had far-reaching effects. . . . The Western empire was poorer and less populous, and its social and economic structure more unhealthy. It was thus less able to withstand the tremendous strains imposed by its defensive effort, and the internal weaknesses which it developed undoubtedly contributed to its final collapse in the fifth century. But the major cause of its fall was that it was more exposed to barbarian onslaughts which in persistence and sheer weight of numbers far exceeded anything which the empire had previously had to face. The Eastern empire, owing to its greater wealth and population and sounder economy, was better able to carry the burden of defense, but its resources were overstrained and it developed the same weaknesses as the West, if perhaps in a less acute form. Despite these weaknesses it managed in the sixth century not only to hold its own against the Persians in the East but to reconquer parts of the West, and even when, in the seventh century, it was overrun by the onslaughts of the Persians and Arabs and the Slavs, it succeeded despite heavy territorial losses in rallying and holding its own. The internal weakness of the empire cannot have been a major factor in its decline.[16]

These remarks show clearly that Jones is not relying exclusively on his East/West comparison to support his claim that increased barbarian pressure was the most important cause of the fall. But I shall continue to consider just what is established by Jones's East/West comparison. Once that is determined, we can consider what the additional arguments add to his case.

In the remarks just quoted, Jones has overstated his case. Even if increased barbarian pressure was "the major cause," that is, the most important cause, of the fall, it does not follow that internal weakness "*cannot* have been *a* major factor." There is conceptual room for more than one important cause of the fall. That nicety aside, the primary obstacle to Jones's concluding anything about causal importance merely on the basis of his East/West comparison is that increased barbarian pressure on the West was not the only cause of the fall that differentiates between the East and the West.

Assume, for instance, that Jones can show, on the basis of his East/West comparison, that the *differentiating* causes of the fall, *taken as a whole*, were more important than non-differentiating causes. That is, assume that Jones can show that those causes of the fall that were present in the West but were not of a kind also present in the East were more important, taken collectively, than all other causes of the fall combined. Even so, nothing would follow concerning the relative importance of any proper subset of these differentiating causes. In particular, nothing would follow concerning the relative importance of increased barbarian pressure on the West.

What then has Jones established merely on the basis of his East/West comparison? The *mere fact* that the East survived while the West collapsed shows that those causes of the fall of a sort present both in the East and in the West were not sufficient for the fall. The *manner in which* the East survived while the West collapsed provides evidence that those causes of the fall that differentiate between East and West, *taken collectively*, were important causes of the fall, that they were, as Jones puts it, more than "a gentle push." Jones has shown nothing, however, about the importance of increased barbarian pressure on the West vis-à-vis any other contributory causes of the fall. Thus, the main burden of showing that increased barbarian pressure on the West was more important than any other cause of the fall must rest on considerations other than Jones's East/West comparison.

Jones argues independently of his East/West comparison that increased barbarian pressure on the West contributed not only directly but also indirectly to the fall. For instance, Jones argues that because of barbarian pressure the Romans significantly increased their army, which, in turn,

> necessitated a rate of taxation so heavy as to cause a progressive decline in agriculture and indirectly a shrinkage of population. The effort to collect this heavy taxation required a great expansion of the civil service, and this expansion in turn imposed an additional burden on the economy and made administrative corruption and extortion more difficult to control. The oppressive weight of the taxation contributed to the general apathy.[17]

The mere fact that increased barbarian pressure on the West contributed both directly and indirectly to the fall cannot be a good reason for concluding that it was the most important cause of the fall or even that it was more important than any other cause. Jones concedes that many so-called "internal causes" of the fall also contributed both directly and indirectly to the fall.[18] And since causes do not always make an equally important direct (or indirect) contribution to a common result, it is possible that the direct (or indirect) contribution of one cause is more important than both the direct and the indirect contributions of another.

Jones's argument that the overall contribution that increased barbarian pressure made to the fall was more important than the contributions of each of the other causes involves a detailed survey of various putative causes of the fall. The point of this survey is to determine, first, the relative importance of each putative cause as a contributory cause of the fall, and, secondly, the relative importance of increased barbarian pressure as a contributory cause of each putative cause. Thus, Jones's main conclusion concerning the relative importance of increased barbarian pressure as a cause of the fall is defended by appeal to various subsidiary conclusions which are also weighted explanations. To understand the argument for Jones's main conclusion one must understand the arguments for Jones's subsidiary conclusions and how these arguments support Jones's main conclusion.

Jones's treatment of putative causes that he denies were contributory causes of the fall is relatively unproblematic. Jones sometimes denies that a putative cause contributed to the fall on the grounds that it is doubtful that the putative cause was present or, even if it was present, that it was efficacious. For example, Jones refutes the arguments of other historians that there was a growth in regional sentiments, a serious decay in trade and industry (excepting agriculture) or a gradual elimination of the "bourgeoisie" or "middle class." He argues that, even if there were a decline in trade or a gradual elimination of the middle class, it is doubtful that these contributed to the fall. Pursuing these particular arguments of his further would not clarify weighted explanations.

Jones's arguments concerning the relative importance of those putative causes of the fall that he admits were both present and efficacious are more to the point. Each such cause of the fall that Jones considers, with one exception, was a change that occurred sometime during the period from the first century A.D. to the fall. This suggests that what Jones has explained is not why Rome fell per se, but rather why it fell in the fifth century when it had not fallen during the Principate or even during the dark days of the third century. His treatment of the exception, to be discussed below, reinforces this impression.

Jones develops his case in a five-stage argument. First, he argues that barbarian pressure on the West increased significantly from the period of the Principate to the time of the fall; hence, the constant reference to "*increased* barbarian pressure" as the most important cause of the fall. Secondly, he downplays the magnitude of other changes which he acknowledges were contributory causes of the fall. For example, he argues that the quality of the army did not deteriorate and that public spirit did not decline as much as some have claimed. Thirdly, he argues that some causes of the fall were not as efficacious as some historians have claimed. For instance, he argues that legislation designed to enforce social regimentation was largely ineffectual. Fourthly, he argues that one particular cause of the fall—the administrative separation of the Eastern and Western parts of the Empire—made a contribution which probably would have been made by something else if the separation had not occurred: it is "doubtful that one man could have effectively controlled both the East and the West in the political and military conditions of the time, when communications were so slow and crises so frequent and sudden. . . . [In a united Empire,] the resources of the eastern parts might have been exhausted, and the West have none the less been lost."[19] Finally, Jones argues that many so-called "internal" causes of the fall were largely the result of increased barbarian pressure; for instance, he argues that barbarian pressure was importantly responsible for growth in administrative corruption and increased taxation, and that increased taxation was importantly responsible for agricultural decline and depopulation: "The burden proved too heavy for agriculture to bear. The higher rate of taxation led to the progressive abandonment of marginal land once cultivated, and many of the peasants, after paying their rents or taxes, had too little food left to rear their children, and the number of producers thus slowly shrank."[20]

Jones's arguments in each of these first three stages address straightforward factual questions of a sort historians routinely address quite apart from their attempts to assess relative causal importance. His arguments in the fourth stage, while relatively unproblematic, will be discussed in the next section. Jones's arguments in the fifth stage raise no new issues: his defense of the subsidiary judgments of relative causal importance consists simply of arguments of the same sorts as those in the first four stages of the strategy now under discussion. The subsidiary judgments themselves are expendable since these judgments do not support his main assessment of relative causal importance beyond the support provided by the evidence for the subsidiary judgments.

Jones does, just once, consider a contributory cause which he acknowledges to be both present and efficacious, but which was not a change that occurred sometime during the period from the first century to the fall. His strategy for dealing with this contributory cause is remarkably different from his strategy for dealing with other causes of the fall. His argument, which follows, bears on the question considered earlier, in our discussion of Dray, of whether weighted explanations are inherently normative:

> The Romans have been criticized for their uninventiveness and lack of enterprise. The economic situation clearly demanded labour saving devices. . . . There existed moreover a fund of theoretical scientific knowledge. . . .
> It is however hardly responsible to single out the Roman empire for criticism on this score. Until the scientific and industrial revolution which began in the eighteenth century, mechanical invention had been in all civilizations excessively rare, and the Romans do not compare unfavorably with the Chinese, the Indians, or with medieval Christendom or Islam.[21]

Jones dismisses "uninventiveness and lack of enterprise" as an important cause of the fall for the blatantly normative reason that it is not "reasonable to single out the Roman empire for criticism on this score." Does this show, then, that Jones is using "more important cause" in a normative sense and that subjectivists such as Dray are right after all? No. It shows only that Jones has in this one instance used "more important cause" in a normative sense. It does not follow that he had to. And since the rest of Jones's argument is clearly an attempt to assess causal importance on factual grounds, it seems more reasonable simply to regard this part of Jones's argument as a mistake.

There is no need for Jones to show that increased barbarian pressure was a more important cause of the fall than "uninventiveness and lack of enterprise." His other arguments support his explanation of why Rome fell during the fifth century when it had not fallen during the previous four. Any contributory causes of Rome's fall, such as "uninventiveness and lack of enterprise," that were present throughout this period may be dismissed on the grounds that they are irrelevant to this explanatory objective. Since "uninventiveness and lack of enterprise" were present also in the East during the period in question, they are irrelevant to explaining why the empire fell during the fifth century in the West, but not in the East. Jones's distinction between more and less important causes of Rome's fall is thus dependent on a prior distinction between causes and conditions. Increased barbarian pressure on the West is not shown to be the most important cause per se of Rome's fall, but rather the most important cause of the fact that Rome fell in the fifth century when it had not fallen during the previous four.

If Jones were not to take this line, then it would be methodologically difficult for him to show that increased barbarian pressure was more important than "uninventiveness and lack of enterprise" as a cause of the fall. I shall explain why below. For now, I should point out that Jones's resort to normative considerations to dispose of this challenge to his conclusion is symptomatic of these methodological difficulties.

What is the status of Jones's argument for the greater relative importance of increased barbarian pressure as a cause of the fall? In the context of comparing the Empire in the West with the Empire in the East, he has established the collective importance of those causes that contributed to the fact that the West collapsed while the East remained strong. He has also provided evidence that barbarian pressure on the West was much greater than barbarian pressure on the East. And he has downplayed the magnitude of other differentiating causes of the fall. Sometimes, as we have seen, he inconsistently asserts that these other differentiating causes were also present to the same degree in the East. In the context of comparing the Empire in the West in the fifth century with the Empire in the West in the first and second centuries, Jones has argued that barbarian pressure was much greater in the fifth century than it had been earlier. His primary strategy with respect to other differentiating causes that he acknowledges were both present and efficacious has been to minimize their magnitude as changes or to argue that increased barbarian pressure was largely responsible for them.

Weighted explanations play a central role in the ways that historians interpret the past. If we knew how to understand the element of causal weighting in such explanations, it would help us to understand how historians defend and how they should defend the comparative superiority of their favored interpretations. So, let us begin by asking what is meant by "more important cause" in Jones's claim that increased barbarian pressure was a more important cause of the fall than any other contributory cause.

It is apparent that Jones has not just asserted his main assessment of relative causal importance, but that he has argued extensively for it. Furthermore, none of his arguments, except for one which we have seen may be disregarded, depend upon appeal to moral considerations or to normative considerations of a sort not present in scientific attempts to defend explanatory claims. These facts are important because they provide a strong prima facie case that Jones's main assessment of relative causal importance is a factual claim.

It is easy to show that there is a factual sense of "more important cause," and that Jones at least once assesses relative causal importance in this sense. Consider the following analysis:

(D1) *A* was a more important cause of *P* relative to Ø than was *B* if
    (1) *A* and *B* were each a cause of *P* relative to Ø, and
    (2) *A* was necessary for *P*, and
    (3) *B* was not necessary for *P*.

In (D1), *A*, *B*, and *P* are placeholders for expressions of the form "the fact that *p*," where *p* is replaced by a full sentence in the indicative mood, for instance, "the fact that the Empire in the West was subjected to barbarian attacks with such and such characteristics during such and such a period," where the "such and suches" are suitably specified. Ø is a placeholder for an expression indicating a comparison-situation, such as "the state of the Empire in the West during the first two centuries A.D."

Item (1) of Analysis (D1) is satisfied just if *A* and *B* are each contributory causes of *P* and factors of a type that differentiates between the situation in which *P* occurred and the comparison-situation Ø—in other words, just if *A* and *B* are at least partial causes, rather than mere conditions, of *P* relative to Ø. The "necessary" in (2) and (3) of (D1) means "necessary under the circumstances." *A* is necessary under the circumstances for *P* just if had *A* had not occurred, then *P* would not have occurred.

Analysis (D1) specifies a logically sufficient condition for an intuitively acceptable sense of "more important cause." Suppose, for instance, that a bill requires fifty-one affirmative votes to pass the U.S. Senate and that on a certain occasion: Senator X votes for the bill—(A_1); Senator Y votes for the bill—(B_1); and the bill receives exactly fifty-one affirmative votes and passes the Senate—(P_1). Suppose further that had Senator X not voted for the bill, the bill would have received only fifty affirmative votes, but that had Senator Y not voted for the bill, then Senator Z, who voted against the bill, would have voted for the bill and the bill would have received exactly fifty-one affirmative votes and passed the Senate. Under these circumstances, A_1, but not B_1, was necessary for P_1. If A_1 and B_1 were each causes of P_1 relative to some comparison-situation, $\emptyset_1$, then in accord with both intuition and (D1), A_1 was a more important cause of P_1 relative to $\emptyset_1$ than was B_1. Jones's claim that many other causes of the fall were more important than the administrative separation of the two parts of the empire may be understood as an instantiation of (D1). Jones argues, in effect, that although administrative separation did contribute to the fall, administrative cohesion would have made a comparable contribution.

It would be a neat victory for objectivity if Jones's main assessment of relative causal importance could be understood as an instantiation of (D1). It cannot. While Jones argues that increased barbarian pressure on the West was a necessary cause of the fall, he does not argue that other causes of the fall were unnecessary. In addition, Jones's supporting arguments would be more effective if his main assessment were interpreted as an instantiation of a different sense of "more important cause." The same is true of virtually all of Jones's subsidiary assessments of relative causal importance.

. Consider the following analysis:[22]

> (D2) A was a more important cause of P relative to $\emptyset$ than was B
> if
> (1) A and B were each a cause of P relative to $\emptyset$, and
> (2) either A was necessary for P or B was not necessary for P, and
> (3) had B not occurred, something would have occurred which more closely approximates P than had A not occurred.

The interpretation of A, B, P, and $\emptyset$ and of (1) and (2) are the same as in Analysis (D1). The interpretation of (3) is problematic, because (3) is a counterfactual, and because the term "more closely approximates" requires clarification.

Although counterfactuals are not well understood, (2) and (3) of (D1) are also counterfactuals, and we saw that (D1) specifies a logically sufficient condition for an intuitively acceptable sense of "more important cause." In addition, many philosophers have shown that counterfactuals, no less problematic or problematic in different ways from (3), are required to explicate a variety of causal and explanatory claims of a sort routinely made by historians and scientists independently of considerations having to do with relative causal importance.[23] Counterfactuals may also be required to explicate other notions, such as "evidence," that we cannot easily abandon.[24] In short, we can often understand counterfactuals well enough to use them, even in philosophical analyses, and, in any case, we seem to be stuck with them. For present purposes, I shall simply assume that we can understand counterfactuals like (3) well enough to use them.[25]

There is a problem with (3), however, that is not a problem with counterfactuals generally, namely, the problem of clarifying "more closely approximates." I shall not define this notion, but only illustrate how it should be understood. It is a familiar and intelligible notion, albeit a vague and problematic one. To the extent that it is intelligible and the illustrations below apt, what follows should provide an acceptable working understanding of (3).

To take the simplest case first, (3) should be understood so that (D1) is just a special case of (D2). Consider again the example used to illustrate (D1). Had Senator Y not voted for the bill, something would have occurred which *more closely approximates* the fact that the bill received exactly fifty-one affirmative votes and passed the Senate than had Senator X not voted for the bill, namely, the bill would have received fifty-one affirmative votes and passed the Senate. Had Senator X not voted for the bill, the bill would have received less than fifty-one affirmative votes and failed to pass the Senate. To revert to symbolism introduced in the initial discussion of this example, had B_1 not occurred, P_1 would have occurred; had A_1 not occurred, P_1 would not have occurred. The occurrence of P_1 more closely approximates P_1 (how close can you get?) than does the non-occurrence of P_1. Thus, substitution instances of (D2) which are also substitution instances of (D1) raise no problems for the interpretation of "more closely approximates."

More problematic substitution instances of (D2) are of two
different kinds. The first measures closeness of approximation in terms of some appropriate quantitative measure. Consider the following variation on the example of the Senate:
Senator X controls a block of five votes; Senator Y controls
only his own vote; had Senator X not voted for the bill, the
bill would have received five fewer affirmative votes than it
did; had Senator Y not voted for the bill, the bill would have
received one less affirmative vote than it did. Given these
suppositions, had Senator Y not voted for the bill, then something would have occurred that more closely approximates
the fact that the bill received at least fifty-one affirmative
votes than had Senator X not voted for the bill. Given that the
other requirements of (D2) are also satisfied, the fact that
Senator X voted for the bill was a more important cause of
the fact that the bill received at least fifty-one affirmative
votes on the occasion in question than was the fact that Senator Y voted for the bill. Some of Jones's subsidiary assessments of relative causal importance seem amenable to this
sort of interpretation, for instance, his claim that poverty was
more important than either plague or barbarian massacres as
a cause of the fact that the peasant population declined below
certain limits.[26]

Sometimes, however, an interpretation of "more closely approximates" will lack the sort of quantitative tidiness of the
examples above and will have to be understood in a non-
quantitative, comparative manner. Jenny is much happier
today than she was last week partly because she passed her
calculus course, but more because her love life has improved.
In this case, we might have reason to say that had Jenny not
passed her calculus course, she would have realized more of
her recent gain in happiness than had her love life not improved, although we could not say, and it may not even make
sense to say, how much more. Similarly, we might have reason
to say that a person's health has deteriorated partly because
of one condition but more because of another, even though
we cannot say, and it may not even make sense to say, how
much more.

These illustrations and explanations are not a systematic account of the meaning of "more closely approximates," but I hope they provide an intuitive understanding clear enough to enable us to determine whether (D2) is or is not satisfied for a wide range of examples. While vague, there is nothing about the notion of "more closely approximates" that suggests that any but factual considerations are relevant to determining which of two possible states more closely approximates an actual state. Suppose, for a given instantiation of (D2), it is not clear which of the counterfactual states postulated more closely approximates P either because it is not clear in the case in question what is meant by "more closely approximates" or because the available evidence does not support either hypothesis better than the other. In such instances, the causes under discussion may not be assigned relative importance in the sense explicated by (D2). However, as the examples above illustrate, often it is clear what is meant by saying that one counterfactual state more closely approximates P than does another, and sometimes it is clear that the available evidence supports one hypothesis better than the other. When these things are sufficiently clear, then the causes under discussion may be weighted in the sense explicated by (D2).

Consider now Jones's main assessment of relative causal importance. If it is *possible* to understand it as an instantiation of (D2), then it must be meaningful to say that various possible states more closely approximate Rome's fall than do other possible states. If it is *plausible* to understand it as an instantiation of (D2), then what Jones correctly provides as evidence for his assessment must be better evidence for it when it is interpreted as an instantiation of (D2) than when it is interpreted in any competing way.

Jones and most other historians of the fall routinely talk in ways which suggest that, in their opinion, it is meaningful to say that some states more closely approximate Rome's fall than do others. This is reflected, for instance, in the hackneyed use of the expression, "the *decline* and fall of Rome" and more generally in the various ways in which Rome's history from the first to the fifth century is characterized as progressive stages of deterioration. Although such talk is neither precise nor perspicuous, it is meaningful. A state that was a more advanced stage of the deterioration that led to Rome's fall than was another state more closely approximates Rome's fall than that other state. Thus, it is possible to understand Jones's main assessment as an instantiation of (D2).

The evidence Jones provides for his main assessment is better evidence for it when the assessment is interpreted as an instantiation of (D2). First, Jones's East/West comparison is an argument for the collective importance of the contributory causes of the fact that the West collapsed while the East remained strong. Secondly, Jones provides evidence that there was greater barbarian pressure on the West than there was on the East, and that the other contributory causes of the fall of the West which differentiate between the East and the West were relatively insignificant deviations from circumstances also present in the East. Finally, Jones provides evidence that tends to show there was a significant increase in barbarian pressure on the West from the first to the fifth century, but that other changes from the first to the fifth century which contributed to the fall were either relatively minor changes, or were ineffectual, or were not necessary causes of the contribution they made to the fall, or were themselves largely the result of increased barbarian pressure.

Jones's evidence for his main assessment is evidence for it because it is evidence for the claims just mentioned. Yet it is hard to imagine how it could be evidence for the claims just mentioned unless it were also evidence for his main assessment when interpreted as an instance of (D2), or at least of some counterfactual analysis closely related to (D2).

It should now be clear why Jones would have had an especially hard time, for methodological reasons, supporting his claim that increased barbarian pressure was a more important cause of the fall than was lack of technical inventiveness. The evidential situation in which Jones finds himself, like those in which most historians find themselves, is such that he is forced to rely heavily on historical comparisons in order to justify his causal claims, including his assessments of relative causal importance. The most useful comparison is usually between the situation in which the result to be explained occurred and other situations in which factors of the same sort as the result were absent. This kind of comparison tends to be more useful the more similar the situations being compared. The most available comparison of this sort and usually the most useful, is with the prior history of the entity whose fate is being explained, in Jones's case, the prior history of the Western part of the Roman Empire. Sometimes a historian is fortunate enough to have another comparison sufficiently similar to be useful. Jones has such a comparison in the circumstances and fate of the Empire in the East.

Jones can say something about what the Western Empire might have been like if barbarian pressure and other causes of the fall had been less acute because there was an earlier time when they were less acute in the Western Empire and a contemporaneous time when they were less acute in the Eastern Empire. It is difficult, however, in the absence of well-confirmed theories of social change of a sort that is not available to historians of the later Roman Empire to judge the relative causal importance of a factor such as "lack of technical inventiveness," which is constant over these comparisons. Moreover, there are no other sufficiently similar comparisons to which Jones might have appealed to support his claim that increased barbarian pressure was more important as a cause of the fall than "lack of technical inventiveness." Hence, Jones's desperate and irrelevant appeal to normative considerations.

I have examined one particular, but complex, example of a historian's argument for a weighted explanation. My examination illustrated the empirical approach to the examination of weighted explanations in history. I believe the way in which the explanation examined was defended is a way good historians often attempt to defend weighted explanations. But I have not shown this and it remains an open question whether it is so. In any case, my examination supports the following theses: First, neither judgments that distinguish causes from conditions, nor judgments that assign relative importance to the causes of particular results, nor the manner in which historians defend either sort of judgment is invariably subjective. Secondly, judgments that distinguish causes from conditions and judgments that assign relative importance to the causes of particular results require radically different analyses. Thirdly, a working understanding of the relationship between these two sorts of judgments is essential to a satisfactory sorting of the central issues involved in at least some significant explanatory controversies in historical studies. And, fourthly, the task of clarifying the manner in which historians assign relative importance to the causes of particular results is an important one, both for historians and for philosophy of history.

The central questions in the philosophical examination of historical explanation are how historians show and how they should show that their explanations are better than competing explanations. The questions of how they show and how they should show that their *weighted* explanations are better than competing weighted explanations are just special cases, though important special cases, of these more general central questions. Although I have not provided final answers to any of these questions, and doubt even that there are final answers, I have suggested preliminary answers to some of them. More importantly, the present chapter and the preceding chapter illustrate the empirical approach to the problem of answering these questions, which has not been tried much in philosophy of history and which differs radically from the conceptual approach that has been in fashion. In my opinion, the only way the central philosophical questions about historical explanation will be answered properly is on the basis of detailed studies of significant instances of actual historical argumentation.

Chapter 5

CONCEPTUAL AND
EMPIRICAL SUBJECTIVISM

I T IS IRONIC that in this century it has tended to be historians who have attacked the objectivity of historical studies and philosophers who have defended it. The historians have argued that historical studies are and always have been subjective, the philosophers that historical studies could in principle be objective.

The debate that first attracted the interest of analytic philosophers was begun by the historians Becker and Beard, who argued that historical studies inescapably are and ought to be done in a way that involves interpretation and conjecture on the part of the historian. Any other approach, they claimed, would trivialize historical studies. To Becker and Beard, this meant that historical studies are and ought to be subjective. The debate that they helped launch evolved in the second half of the century into a debate among historians over the place of social science theory and quantitative methods in historical studies.

Objectivist philosophers changed this primarily methodological debate into a debate over whether historical studies are necessarily subjective, that is, over whether historical studies could in principle be objective, and in so changing the debate, turned away from the empirical examination of historiography and the constraints under which it is written toward a linguistic consideration of the concept of historical studies. In time, even subjectivist philosophers of history tended to assume that the most important philosophical question about the objectivity of historical studies was the objectivist question of whether historical studies are necessarily subjective.

I shall argue below that the question of whether historical studies are necessarily subjective is the wrong primary focus for philosophers interested in the prospects for objectivity in historical studies, and I shall try to redirect philosophical interest toward the questions of whether historical studies are, and are likely to remain subjective, and toward the related questions of how, and at what cost historical studies can be made more objective. As in the discussion of explanation just completed, I shall argue that we philosophers should shift our primary focus away from abstract philosophical possibilities toward concrete historiographical realities. We should stop worrying mainly about understanding the concept of historical studies and turn our attention more fully toward understanding historical studies themselves, that is, we should begin the project of understanding the evidential conventions in terms of which we actually construct historical interpretations.

I want to begin by distinguishing between *conceptual subjectivism*—the view that historical studies, for conceptual reasons, are necessarily subjective, that is, the view that historical studies could not be objective, even in principle—and *empirical subjectivism*—the view that historical studies, for empirical rather than conceptual reasons, are or must be subjective.

Philosophers have understood "subjective" in various senses. Generally they have understood "subjective" to mean "evaluative in a sense of 'evaluative' in which the physical sciences are not evaluative." For now, we can simply leave it an open question exactly what "subjective" means. I shall return below to this question. The important contrasts for now are between *conceptual* and *empirical* versions of the view that historical studies are subjective, and between strong and modest versions of empirical subjectivism. Conceptual subjectivism and strong empirical subjectivism each imply that historical studies are *necessarily* subjective. Modest empirical subjectivism implies only that historical studies *are* subjective. I shall argue that philosophers ought to drop their preoccupation with conceptual subjectivism and with strong empirical subjectivism and focus instead on modest empirical subjectivism.

First, consider conceptual subjectivism, the view that historical studies, for conceptual reasons, are necessarily subjective. To say that historical studies are necessarily subjective, as I shall understand "necessarily," is to say that it is conceptually impossible for something to be a historical study and not be subjective. In other words, it is to say that given certain definitions, or partial definitions, of "historical studies" and "subjective," it is logically impossible for something to be a historical study and not be subjective.

This way of understanding "necessarily," as it occurs in the claim that historical studies are necessarily subjective, is, I think, the central way in which philosophers have understood it during this century and still understand it today. Consider, for instance, the following remarks of William Dray in his widely read introduction to philosophy of history:

> The interest of critical philosophy of history in this matter will clearly not be to discover simply whether history, as generally pursued, is *in fact* a value-neutral inquiry. The question will be rather whether it is so in concept or "idea." . . . For if value judgment is logically ingredient in the very idea of historical inquiry, it would make no sense for historians even to *aspire* to be objective.[1]

Dray is assuming, for the sake of argument, that value judgments are subjective. But what is important, for present purposes, is Dray's view that the philosophically significant question is whether historical studies are necessarily subjective, and that how this question is answered depends on whether there is a conceptual or logical link between the notion of "historical studies" and the notions of "evaluative," and hence of "subjective," inquiry. In other words, Dray seems to be understanding "necessarily" just as I have defined it in the remarks above.

This is not the only way in which "necessarily" has been understood by those who have argued that historical studies are necessarily subjective. There is another, less central, but still important understanding—that historical studies are necessarily subjective just if there is an empirical law of nature which guarantees that anything that is a historical study is

subjective. That there is such a law is the central claim of
strong empirical subjectivism. To avoid confusing these two
senses of "necessarily," let us say that a historical study that is
necessarily subjective in the more central sense, the sense in
which I want now to understand "necessarily," is "conceptu-
ally-necessarily" subjective, whereas a historical study that is
necessarily subjective in the less central sense just specified is
"empirically-necessarily" subjective. I shall discuss the claim
that historical studies are empirically-necessarily subjective
later, and so shall say no more about it here. For the time
being, let us understand "necessarily" to mean "conceptually-
necessarily."

Those who have tried to show that historical studies are
necessarily subjective have usually tried to show that historical studies are subjective in a sense of "subjective" in which
the physical sciences are not necessarily subjective. I shall
confine my discussion to such arguments. A problem with
most such arguments is that the characterizations of physical
science on which they depend are usually derived from logical positivism, and most philosophers now feel that logical
positivism does not give a satisfactory account of physical
science. The points that I want to make are independent of
this sort of complication.

I assume that no one has ever argued successfully that
historical studies are necessarily subjective. Certainly no argument that anyone has ever proposed has won anything like
widespread support even within the philosophy of history.
Objectivist counterarguments have been more than sufficient
to dismantle subjectivist attempts to show that historical studies are necessarily subjective. The major objectivist counterarguments are well known and tend to be repeated over and
over.[2] They follow a common pattern. Objectivists typically
catalogue the characteristics of historical studies that subjectivists have cited as proof that historical studies are necessarily subjective, for instance, that they are selective. They then
show for each of these characteristics either that it is not
necessarily a characteristic of historical studies, or that while
it may necessarily be a characteristic of historical studies, it is
also necessarily a characteristic of science, or else that while

the characteristic cited may necessarily be a characteristic of historical studies, but not of science, it is not a characteristic that makes historical studies subjective.

I do not wish to rehearse here the subjectivist arguments and the objectivist replies. What I want to do instead is *explain* why no one has ever argued successfully that historical studies are necessarily subjective, and explain it in a way that will break the attraction—for both subjectivists and objectivists—to this aspect of the question of historical objectivity. That is, I want to try to move the discussion, in stages, from a debate over the question of whether historical studies are necessarily subjective to a consideration of whether historical studies are and are likely to remain subjective. The way to do that, I believe, is for us to clarify what it takes to show that historical studies are necessarily subjective.

To argue successfully that historical studies are necessarily subjective, one must both construct an argument that establishes that they are *and* also show that the conclusion of that argument is important. No one has ever done both of these things. More importantly, no one seems to have realized how easy it is to do the former and how hard it is to do the latter.

An argument that historical studies are necessarily subjective establishes its conclusion only if its premises logically imply, or entail, its conclusion. All such arguments have, or can be recast to have, the following form:

(1) It is necessarily the case that something is a historical study only if it has feature S_1.
(2) It is necessarily the case that something has feature S_1 only if it is subjective.

Therefore, (3) it is necessarily the case that something is a historical study only if it is subjective.

I shall consider an argument to have this form even if its version of premise (2) may be expanded at whatever length along the following lines:

(2.1) It is necessarily the case that something has feature S_1 only if it has feature S_2.
(2.2) It is necessarily the case that something has feature S_2 only if it has feature S_3.

(2.n) It is necessarily the case that something has feature S_n only if it is subjective.

Thus, for instance, the argument that follows is of the form under discussion:

(4) It is necessarily the case that something is a historical study only if it includes selective causal judgments.

(5) It is necessarily the case that something includes selective causal judgments only if it includes or implies moral judgments.

(6) It is necessarily the case that something includes or implies moral judgments only if it is subjective.

Therefore, (7) it is necessarily the case that something is a historical study only if it is subjective.

This argument from (4), (5), and (6), to (7) is valid, that is, (7) follows logically from (4), (5), and (6). If we assume, for the sake of argument, that (4), (5), and (6) are true, then the argument is also sound. But it is not thereby a successful argument. It is successful only if its conclusion is important. Its conclusion is that historical studies are necessarily subjective. That may seem like an important conclusion. But is it really?

Given the way I am understanding "necessarily," it is a truism that whether historical studies are necessarily subjective all depends on what one understands by "historical studies" and by "subjective." And it is an obvious fact that the expressions "historical studies" and "subjective" are ambiguous. Thus, the claim that historical studies are necessarily subjective is also ambiguous unless an unambiguous sense is specified for "historical studies" and "subjective."

We have defined "necessarily." Thus, whether historical studies are necessarily subjective all depends on what we mean by "historical studies" and by "subjective." In some senses of "historical studies" and "subjective" the answer may be yes, in others no. The claim that historical studies are necessarily subjective, when formulated unambiguously, means that historical studies are necessarily subjective in certain specified senses of "historical studies" and "subjective," a claim which, if true, leaves open the possibility that there are other senses of "historical studies" and "subjective" in which it may not be true that historical studies are necessarily subjective.

It should now be clear why it is extremely easy to prove that historical studies are necessarily subjective in the only way in which one can prove that historical studies are necessarily subjective: by specifying definitions, or partial definitions, of "historical studies," "subjective," and perhaps related expressions, such as "evaluative," from which it follows logically that something is a historical study only if it is subjective.

The point may be put a little differently. Two things, and two things only, must be shown in order to establish that historical studies are necessarily subjective: first, that some characteristic is essential to historical studies, that is, that every historical study, in order even to qualify as a historical study, must include this characteristic; and secondly, that this characteristic is essentially subjective. But we have no magical access to the "essence" of historical studies. Our only access is through the definition of words. We may wish to argue that the definitions we favor are ones that are currently in use, but that argument cannot establish that we should stick to that current usage.

The only way to establish that a certain characteristic is essential to historical studies is simply to define the expression, "historical studies," so that it is conceptually impossible for something to be a historical study and not include that characteristic. Having done that, one must show that the characteristic in question is essentially subjective in order to show that historical studies are necessarily subjective. But this too is a definitional task. As we can see, for instance, if we consider the argument (4) through (7) above, the mere fact that historians have made selective causal judgments that *are* evaluative does not and cannot show that a selective causal judgment *must be* evaluative. In sum, if a version of *conceptual* subjectivism is true, it is true by definition.

One may define "historical studies" and the sorts of characteristics that are said to be essential to historical studies in a great variety of ways. However one defines these terms, empirical evidence is irrelevant to the justification of these definitions, if it even makes sense to speak of definitions being justified. Thus, empirical evidence is irrelevant to the justification of conceptual subjectivism.

Since the justification of conceptual subjectivism consists simply in its deduction from definitions, conceptual subjectivism as such is easily established, but potentially trivial. Those who find this counterintuitive are probably confusing the justification of some version of conceptual subjectivism with the justification of the importance of that version of conceptual subjectivism. To show that a version of conceptual subjectivism is important, one would have to show that the definitions upon which it is based are important definitions, and one can do that only by showing that the definitions are appropriately related to important descriptive or explanatory aims of historians. But this may be—indeed, will be—hard to do.

Suppose, to return to the argument (4) through (7), that "historical studies" is defined so that nothing is a historical study unless it includes or implies a selective causal judgment, and the latter is defined so that nothing is a selective causal judgment unless it implies an evaluative judgment. A version of conceptual subjectivism follows from these definitions. Suppose further that one attempts to show the importance of this version of conceptual subjectivism by illustrating the ubiquity of selective causal judgments, in the sense defined, in historical accounts that are generally acknowledged to be important contributions to historiography. This strategy, as we have seen, leaves open the possibility that "selective causal judgment" might be redefined in some non-evaluative way and that selective causal judgment, so redefined, is as adequate as, or more adequate than, selective causal judgment in its essentially evaluative sense to the descriptive and explanatory aspirations of historians. Unless the possibility of such redefinition is eliminated, or the importance of selective causal judgment that is essentially evaluative to some important non-descriptive and non-explanatory aspiration of historians—say, some moral or aesthetic goal—is shown, the importance of the version of subjectivism under consideration will not have been established.[3]

William Dray, for instance, tries to show that the causal judgments which historians make are typically, if not always, evaluative in that they are "logically dependent on," and not merely causally influenced by, the historian's moral judgments.[4] Dray supports this thesis by an examination of alternative interpretations of the American Civil War. He concludes that the evaluative character of the causal judgments embedded in these interpretations explains "why historians will never know 'objectively' what caused the Civil War—why, in Stampp's words, 'after a century of enormous effort, the debate is still inconclusive.' "[5]

The problem, as Dray sees it, is that the historian's causal judgments are "selective," that is, they require that the historian distinguish between causes and conditions. Dray believes this distinction is an evaluative distinction. For instance, Dray argues that when a historian is faced with the problem of deciding whether a problematic situation or an agent's response to that situation is the cause of some result to which both contributed, the historian's decision depends on a moral assessment of the situation under consideration. In the case of historians of the American Civil War, a "conflict theorist," for instance, "selects the predicament itself as cause because he judges that no course of action that could reasonably have been expected by the men of either side would have succeeded in avoiding war."[6]

Let us assume with Dray that selective causal judgment is essential to historical studies. Dray argues that the selective causal judgments of historians are evaluative by showing that historians often use evaluative considerations as evidence for these judgments. But Dray has neither shown nor attempted to show that a non-evaluative principle of selection for such judgments is impossible or that one would not suit the descriptive and explanatory purposes of historians as well as, or better than, an evaluative principle of selection. In other words, even if the selective causal judgments of historians are evaluative, it does not follow that they must be evaluative. To establish that historical studies are necessarily subjective in the way Dray is trying to establish it, he would have to show that selective causal judgments must be evaluative. But how can Dray ever show that such judgments *must* be evaluative on the basis of a historiographical survey? The answer: he cannot.[7]

It is not easy to stipulate definitions that imply conceptual subjectivism and are appropriately related to the explanatory or descriptive aims of some important group of historians. The reason is that such definitions are appropriately related only if they are not vulnerable to redefinition of the sort just indicated. To my knowledge, such definitions have never been stipulated. Hence, I do not believe that any version of conceptual subjectivism for which philosophers or historians have ever argued has been shown to be important.

Since it is so easy to prove that historical studies are necessarily subjective and so questionable whether in doing so one has done something important, one might expect that serious attempts to show that historical studies are necessarily subjective would consist of two parts: short, snappy, definition-dependent arguments that historical studies are necessarily subjective, followed by more elaborate arguments that what one has shown is important. In fact, I know of no argument that historical studies are necessarily subjective that is organized in this way, despite an extensive literature on the question. The ways in which such arguments are organized often reveal considerable confusion over how, if at all, one can prove that historical studies are necessarily subjective.

What of the view that historical studies are empirically-necessarily subjective, that is, the view that historical studies must be subjective, but in an empirical rather than a conceptual sense of "must"? This is the view that historical studies are subjective as a consequence of natural law or of something closely approximating natural law.

The claim that historical studies are empirically-necessarily subjective does not imply that a historical study cannot conceivably be objective, but it is a strong and interesting thesis nevertheless, and it is a thesis that sometimes seems, among historians at least, to be part of the common wisdom about historical studies. Beard, for instance, once challenged those who believe that historical studies can be objective to produce an objective historical study. And some who do not claim that an objective historical study is conceptually impossible nevertheless claim that an objective historical study is "humanly impossible."

We have already seen that we cannot show empirically that historical studies are *conceptually*-necessarily subjective. Can we show empirically that they are *empirically*-necessarily subjective? We could if we were able to show that certain circumstances always have been and always will be present whenever historical studies are composed and that these circumstances guarantee that historical studies include some characteristic, such as an evaluative judgment, that makes historical studies subjective. But are we able to show this?

Empirically grounded arguments that historical studies must be subjective inevitably face the accusation that they are "self-refuting." This accusation is then used as a way of dismissing this version of subjectivism. The same sort of move occurs in philosophy of science and in discussions of relativism generally. For instance, ever since the publication, in 1962, of Thomas Kuhn's *The Structure of Scientific Revolutions*, it has been fashionable to argue on historical grounds that the physical sciences are subjective. But historically grounded arguments for the subjectivity of the physical sciences are puzzling and controversial, not the least because they seem both to call into question and to presuppose the objectivity of historical studies.[8] Some critics have focused on this aspect of historically grounded arguments for the subjectivity of science to argue that such arguments are necessarily self-refuting. Israel Scheffler, for instance, has noted what he takes to be

> the striking self-contradictoriness that infects arguments for such a view, when they themselves appeal, by way of rational justification, to the hard realities of the history of science.[9]

Scheffler remarks that "if *historians* can transcend particular paradigms and evaluate them by appeal to neutral evidence, so can *scientists*. . . ."[10] Scheffler would have even stronger reason to argue that any historically grounded argument to show that *historical studies* must be subjective is necessarily self-refuting.

I shall argue that historically grounded arguments that historical studies must be subjective are *not* necessarily self-refuting. If I am right, then *a fortiori* the accusation of self-refutation cannot be sustained against historically grounded arguments that science is subjective. However, my ultimate objective is not to defend strong empirical subjectivism, but rather to show what is really wrong with it. We can best see what is wrong with it if we first set aside the suspicion that all empirically grounded arguments that historical studies must be subjective are necessarily self-refuting.

There are as many versions of the claim that historical studies are or must be subjective as there are ways of understanding "subjective." But there are two versions, which I shall call "evaluativism" and "skepticism," that have been more central than any others in the important twentieth-century literature on the subjectivity of historical studies. According to evaluativism, certain kinds of claims that are essential to historical studies are evaluative (as opposed to "factual" or "merely factual"). Ethical claims have received the most discussion, but aesthetic claims and a great many claims that do not fall neatly under any evaluative label are also relevant.[11] According to skepticism, certain kinds of claims that are essential to historical studies are incapable of being justified. A kind of claim is incapable of being justified just in case, roughly, it is impossible to show that one claim of that kind is better supported by evidence than some other claim of that kind that is incompatible with it. For instance, if weighted explanations are essential to historical studies, and if the weighting aspect of such explanations is always "arbitrary," as some have argued, then a kind of claim which is essential to historical studies is incapable of being justified, and skepticism must therefore be true.[12]

Evaluativism and skepticism are not mutually exclusive. In fact, one reason discussion of evaluative claims has been central to the debate over whether historical studies are or must be subjective is that it is widely assumed, particularly by historians, that evaluative claims are incapable of being justified. Most who have argued for evaluativism have been interested in establishing skepticism, and have assumed that evaluativism implies skepticism. For present purposes, we need not consider whether this assumption is true.

Our question is this: are historically grounded arguments that historical studies must be subjective necessarily self-refuting? The best argument that they are is suggested by Ernest Nagel's reply to E. H. Carr's suggestion, "Before you study the history, study the historian. . . . Before you study the historian, study his historical and social environment."[13] Nagel replies that "we must at some point judge the factual worth of a historical reconstruction without first studying the historian and his environment (and hence must reject the version of relativism under discussion), or else embark upon an infinite regress whose only fruit is a skepticism so thoroughgoing that *it destroys even the ground upon which this form of historical relativism is asserted to rest*."[14]

Carr's suggestion provoked a similar reaction from Sidney Hook: "With explicit reference to Gibbon he [Carr] tells us that the point of view of a historian, his basic values and explanatory categories, are more likely to 'reflect the period in which he lives than the period about which he writes.' " Hook claims that Carr's view "cannot be generalized without inconsistency."

> When Carr says of Gibbon that he reflects the eighteenth century rather than the centuries of the Roman Empire, how does he know this? Is he not clearly implying that he knows truly what the thoughts, sentiments and judgments of the eighteenth century are? But if one were to apply his own maxim to his observations on Gibbon would one not be justified in saying that what Carr believes about the eighteenth century reflects the twentieth century more than the eighteenth? And if this is so, how can Carr confidently assert that Gibbon is giving us an inadequate account of Rome or one less adequate than of the eighteenth century? To make sense of his observation in this particular case, Carr must claim that he knows the relevant truth about Rome and the relevant truth about Gibbon's England and that Gibbon couldn't see

the truth about Rome because he wrote with the blinders of the eighteenth century—something which is apparent to Carr because *he* writes without the blinders of the twentieth century.[15]

It is arguable that Carr is not committed to the view that Nagel and Hook are criticizing. For present purposes it does not matter. What does matter is that both Nagel and Hook have given us seemingly persuasive reasons why historically grounded arguments for skepticism are necessarily self-refuting. Are these reasons good reasons?

How might a skeptic reply? To make things as tidy as possible, consider the case of an *extreme* skeptic, one who argues on historical grounds that *no* historical claim can be justified. If the historically grounded arguments of an extreme skeptic are necessarily self-refuting, the arguments of less extreme skeptics still may not be. But if extreme skeptics do not necessarily refute themselves, it is doubtful that less extreme skeptics, much less all those who argue on historical grounds that historical studies must be subjective, necessarily refute themselves.

The best argument to show that the arguments of an extreme skeptic are necessarily self-refuting seems to be the following:

(11) Some historical claims are non-redundant premises in the extreme skeptic's argument. [Premise (11) is true *ex hypothesi.*]

(12) If these historical claims are justified, the extreme skeptic's conclusion is false. [The skeptic's conclusion is that no historical claim can be justified.]

(13) If these historical claims are not justified, the extreme skeptic's conclusion is not justified. [Some of the requisite premises in the skeptic's argument have not been justified.]

Therefore, (14) the extreme skeptic's conclusion is either false or unjustified.

Therefore, (15) the extreme skeptic's argument is self-refuting, that is, the premises of his argument are justified only if his conclusion is either false or unjustified.

This argument is independent of any accidental features of extreme skepticism, and it is valid. If each premise is necessarily true, it shows that the extreme skeptic's attempt to argue on historical grounds that historical studies must be subjective is necessarily self-refuting. The question, then, is whether each premise is necessarily true.

While the argument just presented helps to explain why subjectivists are often labeled "inconsistent," it does not show that the extreme skeptic is committed to an explicit inconsistency. The extreme skeptic has employed historical claims in his argument and has concluded that no historical claim can be justified. But there is no explicit inconsistency in that. One might contend (see Hook) that in employing historical claims as premises in his argument the extreme skeptic must *implicitly* be claiming that some historical claims are justified. And the claim that some historical claims are justified is explicitly inconsistent with the extreme skeptic's contention that no historical claims are justified. But it is difficult to see how this view about the extreme skeptic's implicit claims can itself be justified, since it depends on the false assumption that the author of an argument must claim that every premise in his argument is justified.

One can use a premise in an argument without asserting it. For instance, one can argue for a conclusion via a *reductio ad absurdum* of the plausible or accepted alternatives to that conclusion. In a reductio, one assumes that certain premises are true for the purpose of showing that they, perhaps together with other premises which are asserted, have an unacceptable implication. The author of a reductio is obviously not committed to claiming of the premises that he assumes they are either justified or true since the whole point of the reductio is to show that they are not.

An extreme skeptic's argument for subjectivism may be construed as a reductio. It is enough for the skeptic's purposes if the historical claims employed as premises in his arguments are justified on the basis of his objectivist opponent's criteria for the justification of such claims. The skeptic need not imply that the historical claims employed as premises in his argument are justified in any stronger sense, in particular, he need not imply that they are justified per se. The skeptic is entitled to employ certain premises, which he does not think or imply are justified, in arguments against objectivists who believe these premises are justified. Hence, premise (13) of the argument above is not necessarily true.

The extreme skeptic's argument may fail, nonetheless, in any number of ways. His historical premises may not be justified on the basis of objectivist criteria of justification. One of his non-historical premises may be false or unjustified. His premises, even if they are all true, may not imply his conclusion. My point is simply that the refutation above of extreme skepticism does not work. It does not show either that the skeptic is committed to an inconsistency, or that the skeptic cannot provide an objectivist with good reasons for accepting the skeptic's conclusion, or that the skeptic cannot have good reasons for accepting his own conclusion. Thus, the extreme skeptic's argument has not been shown to be necessarily self-refuting.

I do not know of any skeptic who has argued on historical grounds for subjectivism and has explicitly claimed to be merely assuming, rather than asserting, the historical premises in his argument. My point is not that any skeptic has claimed this, but rather that a skeptic could claim this of his historical premises. The question at issue is whether historically grounded arguments that historical studies must be subjective are *necessarily* self-refuting, not whether the arguments of some particular subjectivist are as a matter of fact self-refuting.[16] The answer seems to be that historically grounded arguments that historical studies must be subjective are not necessarily self-refuting.

I have shown how a subjectivist could argue on historical grounds that historical studies must be subjective and avoid self-refutation if his argument were a reductio. But there are also other ways to avoid self-refutation. The problem of self-refutation does not even arise for a subjectivist who argues for evaluativism, but denies skepticism. The most we can conclude of such a subjectivist is that some or all of his historical claims are evaluative. But if he asserts that evaluative claims are capable of being justified,[17] or simply leaves it an open question whether they are capable of being justified,[18] then we cannot conclude, from the supposition that some of his premises are evaluative, that he has refuted himself. Even if a subjectivist argues on historical grounds for skepticism, the historical premises in his argument may not be instances of the kind of claim essential to history that he says is incapable of being justified. Thus, even a skeptic who asserts, rather than merely assumes, the historical premises in his argument for subjectivism may avoid self-refutation.

Strong empirical subjectivism, that is, the claim that historical studies are empirically-necessarily subjective, resembles the claim that all men are mortal. While it is conceivable that a human never experiences bodily death and that a historical study is objective, many do not regard either as a "real possibility." Both claims share some of the distinguishing characteristics of general causal claims, for instance, both sustain the relevant subjunctive conditionals.[19] Yet both claims have minimal explanatory value. To know simply that all men are mortal is not to know what it is about the way human bodies function and deteriorate that insures mortality. Similarly, to know simply that historical studies are subjective is not to know what it is about the way historical studies are composed that insures they are subjective.

To show that historical studies are empirically-necessarily subjective, one must at least show that circumstances that are and always will be present whenever historical studies are composed guarantee the inclusion in each historical study of some characteristic that makes historical studies subjective. Given the practical difficulties of any sort of experimental confirmation of a claim such as this, it is likely that evidence that is based on historical or sociological data collected largely, if not entirely, independently of experimentation would play a crucial role in confirming it. Certainly the evidence that exists at the present time, such as the sort of evidence assembled by sociologists of knowledge, is almost exclusively non-experimental.

The claim that it is impossible for a historical study to be objective does not easily lend itself to empirical test, even of a very informal sort. This problem is related to the claim's lack of explanatory value. That it is humanly impossible for a historical study to be objective does not explain, for instance, why objectivity in a historical study cannot be achieved

on a small scale, say, in cases when the "historical study" is a
sentence or a paragraph long. Consider, for instance, the following "historical study": Abraham Lincoln was shot by John
Wilkes Booth at Ford's Theater in Washington, D.C. Is this
"historical study" objective or not?

The claim that it is impossible for historical studies to be
objective does not explain why the "historical study" just
given could not be objective. Nor does it explain—assuming
that the "historical study" just given can be objective, but does
not qualify as a historical study—what precludes the possibility of expanding it, sentence by sentence, without compro-
mising its objectivity, to the point where it does qualify as a
historical study? To be convinced that historical studies are
empirically-necessarily subjective we shall have to know at
what point and why in the process of such a sentence-by-
sentence expansion of a proto-historical account it ceases to
be objective and becomes subjective.

Attempts by subjectivists to be more specific about their
claim that historical studies are empirically-necessarily subjective, and thereby to enhance the empirical status of this claim
and increase its explanatory value, have not been successful.
For example, it is sometimes said that it is a historian's subjective bias—say, her "ideological commitment" or her "cultural
bias"—that insures that historical studies will be subjective.
Hence, we *are* told, albeit vaguely, what it is about being a
historian or composing a historical study that insures that
historical studies will be subjective. But we are never, so far
as I know, given clear directions for distinguishing the presence of subjective bias from its absence. The most that is done
is the detection of the presence of subjective bias in some
particular historian or in all historians who write from a
specific, but not universally shared, point of view.[20] Equally
important, we are never given good reasons for believing that
all historians have had and will continue to have a subjective
bias. But to show in this way that historical studies are empirically-necessarily subjective, one must show that all historians
have had and will have a subjective bias and that there is a
correlation between their having such a bias and their making
a kind of subjective judgment that is essential to their historical studies.

Little has been done to show in a general way that a subjective bias, when present, inevitably compromises the objectivity of a historian's work or how this occurs. Even commentators otherwise sympathetic with the sociology of knowledge movement sometimes bemoan the failure of those who claim that historical studies are subjective to provide a "mechanism," that is, roughly, an explanation of the purported correlation between subjective bias and kinds of subjective judgments included in historical accounts.[21] In the absence of such explanations, we shall never know why proto-historical accounts of the sort provided above could not be objective or progressively expanded into objective historical studies. And if we do not know this, we do not know that historical studies must be subjective.

Is there a fruitful philosophical question about the subjectivity of historical studies? Yes, there is the question simply of whether historical studies *are* subjective. And if they are subjective, there are the related questions of whether they are likely to remain subjective and of whether various ways in which they could be made more objective are worth the cost. Dray, for instance, could have framed his argument, which we considered above, so that it is directly responsive to such questions. He could have argued that the vast majority of selective causal judgments in historical accounts are evaluative, not because they have to be, but simply because of the evaluative bases on which they are made. Dray could have argued for this modest version of empirical subjectivism by appealing, just as he did, to the kinds of reasons historians give in defense of their selective causal judgments. If Dray had argued in this way, he could not have concluded that it does not make sense for historians to aspire to be objective. Rather, his arguments would have raised the questions of whether and how historians could have been more objective and of whether it would have been worth the cost.

I have distinguished three versions of subjectivism and considered the question of what it would take to show that they are true. We have seen that while conceptual subjectivists can easily establish that historical studies are necessarily subjective, it is unlikely that in doing so they will have established anything that is important. We have also seen that while strong empirical subjectivists argue for an important conclusion, it is unlikely that they can establish it. That leaves modest empirical subjectivism, which claims only that historical studies have been, and perhaps are likely to remain, subjective. Modest empirical subjectivists are more likely than strong empirical subjectivists to establish their conclusions, and their conclusions are more likely than those of conceptual subjectivists to be important. If modest empirical subjectivists establish that historical studies are subjective, they not only shed light on historical studies, they also raise the question of whether historical methodology should be changed. Their rhetoric is less pretentious than the rhetoric of conceptual subjectivists or strong empirical subjectivists, but they are talking about real historical studies, rather than simply the idea of historical studies, and what they say about historical studies is much more likely to be useful.

Chapter 6

MODEST EMPIRICAL
SUBJECTIVISM

T HE IDEA that a good historian often can assess the relative likelihood of competing historical claims more reliably on implicit grounds—intuitively, if you like—than in any other available way has been a persistent theme of *Verstehen*-theorists. It is, in essence, the old saw that there is no substitute for the brewmaster's nose, adapted to the art of producing historical brew. If true, it augments the importance of the historian relative to his arguments, and thereby gives him a dignity he might otherwise lack. Some have thought that it marks an important methodological difference between historical studies and the natural sciences. It is, in its way, a humane idea. But is it true?

Historians do history as if the idea were true. That is, they often argue for their solutions to historical problems in ways that support their solutions only if the idea were true. But are they entitled to argue in these ways? Standard objections to the use of *Verstehen* as a technique of confirmation in historical studies imply that they are not.[1] However, I shall argue, first, that historians are often entitled to argue in these ways, that is, that *Verstehen* of a sort is a legitimate technique of confirmation in historical studies, and, secondly, that the extent to which historians argue in these ways may well mark an important methodological difference between historical studies and the natural sciences.

The traditional debate over the place of *Verstehen* in historical studies is really a syndrome of many debates, only some of which concern the use of *Verstehen* as a technique of confirmation. These latter debates, when they are not relatively arid debates over the meaning of words such as "evidence," "knowledge," or "science," are most fundamentally debates over how history ought to be done, that is, over how we can most responsibly construct and evaluate historical interpretations.

The standard criticism of *Verstehen* is that while it may have heuristic value as a source of hypotheses, it has no value as a technique of confirmation. But those who urge this criticism show only that there are important limitations to *Verstehen* as a technique of confirmation, not that there is a realistic alternative. Hence, the standard criticism is methodologically sterile, for there is no methodological point in insisting on the limitations of a technique for achieving some objective if we are committed to pursuing that objective and that technique is the best means available to achieve it. At most, the standard criticism will affect how we view the results of using *Verstehen*. I shall consider the standard criticism first, and then return to this related point.

Consider, for instance, the argument in Theodore Abel's classic paper, "The Operation Called *Verstehen*," in which Abel examines three confirmational uses to which *Verstehen* has been put, then analyzes what "the operation of *Verstehen*" involves, and argues against the value of *Verstehen* as a technique of confirmation. I can convey the relevant part of Abel's argument by considering just his discussion of the first of his three examples:

> Last April 15 a freezing spell suddenly set in, causing a temperature drop from 60 to 34 degrees. I saw my neighbor rise from his desk by the window, walk to the woodshed, pick up an ax, and chop some wood. I then observed him carrying the wood into the house and placing it in the fireplace. After he had lighted the wood, he sat down at his desk and resumed his daily task of writing.
>
> From these observations I concluded that, while working, my neighbor began to feel chilly and, in order to get warm, lighted a fire.[2]

Abel notes that this explanation of his neighbor's behavior *may not* be correct, even though it "has all the earmarks of an obvious fact.' "

To be sure my explanation is correct, I need additional information. I can go over to him and ask him why he lighted the fire. He may confirm my interpretation. However, I cannot stop there. Suppose he has another, hidden, intention? He may be expecting a guest and wish to show off his fireplace. Or suppose he himself is not aware of the "true" motive? Perhaps he was impelled by a subconscious motive of wanting to burn down his house so as to punish the fellow who harasses him about paying off the mortgage.[3]

Abel has reminded us that the original explanation *might* be wrong. But how does he move from this rather bland observation to his extreme conclusion that one is not entitled, in the absence of "additional information," to infer that the original explanation is nevertheless *probably* correct?

Abel's analysis of the operation of *Verstehen* provides the missing steps:

Two sets of observations are given in our example. First, there is a sequence of bodily movement (chopping wood, lighting a fire, etc.); second, there is a thermometer reading of a near-freezing temperature. The act of *Verstehen* links these two facts into the conclusion that the freezing weather was the stimulus which set off the response "making a fire."[4]

Verstehen, on Abel's view, involves an "internalization" of certain observed conditions which are then "linked together" via a "behavior maxim," in this case the generalization that "a person 'feeling cold' will 'seek warmth.' "

Abel's basic criticism of *Verstehen* is that its use presupposes the truth of generalizations which have not been shown to be true and probably cannot be shown to be true. In the present example, two of the three generalizations involve the "internalization" of the observed conditions. Abel complains that these generalizations are formed in the absence of "specific techniques. . . . which permit a definite association between feeling-states and observed behavior," and that the procedures we employ to "internalize" these observed conditions are "arbitrary." The third generalization is the "behavior maxim." Abel's objection to behavior maxims is that they "are not recorded in any textbooks on human behavior . . . they have not been established experimentally."[5]

Abel concludes that these limitations on the operation of *Verstehen* "virtually preclude" its use "as a scientific tool of analysis." *Verstehen* may relieve "us of a sense of apprehension in connection with behavior that is unfamiliar or unexpected and it is a source of 'hunches' which help us in the formulation of hypotheses." But *Verstehen* does not give us knowledge "nor does it serve as a means of verification. The *probability* of a connection can be ascertained only by means of objective, experimental, and statistical tests."[6]

The main problem with Abel's account and criticisms— which are strikingly reminiscent of Murphey's account and criticisms of the way historians typically defend their explanatory claims—is that Abel has underestimated the value of *Verstehen* in circumstances where there is no better alternative. Reconsider his example. This time, imagine that you observed your neighbor do the things Abel describes, and that, in order to achieve some worthwhile objective, you had to explain your neighbor's behavior by choosing among just those explanations that Abel mentions. Suppose further that you could not conduct an investigation or gather additional information and that your background knowledge is of a conventional sort—you know your neighbor's house is a normal house inhabited by normal people, and so on. Under these circumstances a rational person would opt for Abel's initial explanation, the one that he says has "all the earmarks of an 'obvious fact.' " But Abel can provide no basis for this preference. Any of the three explanations could be true. And Abel stresses that from the point of view of *Verstehen* alone, any connection that is possible is equally probable, and "the test of the actual probability calls for the application of objective methods of observation: e.g. experiments, comparative studies, statistical operations of mass data, etc."[7] So, on Abel's view, someone who is unable to conduct such tests has no rational basis for choosing among the three explanations. Since it is obvious that a rational person with background knowledge of a conventional sort would not choose randomly among the three explanations, but would instead opt for the original explanation, there must be something wrong with Abel's view.

Historians are often faced with the task of choosing among competing explanations in the absence of what Abel would regard as "objective methods of observation." In doing so they must presuppose the truth of certain generalizations (not necessarily of the same sort that Abel mentions), which are at least impractical, if not impossible, to confirm. The most rational procedure available to historians in such circumstances is often to rely on their educated judgment to choose among competing explanations. This observation is humdrum if those cases where historians may rely on their educated judgment are cases where they could, if challenged, back up their claims without relying on their judgment. Legitimate *Verstehen*, then, would be just an innocuous, laborsaving device. But what of cases where historians cannot back up their claims without relying on their judgment? Do good historians often rely on their judgment in such cases? May they? I suggest that they do, and that they may.

I want now to look in detail at a significant historical controversy in order to clarify and illustrate the idea that historians often rely on arguments that depend essentially on historical judgments; that is, they rely on arguments that depend on historical judgments that they cannot defend without relying on other arguments that also depend on historical judgments. Consideration of this idea within the context of an actual historical controversy will connect our theoretical discussion to the details of historical study and also illustrate the empirical approach to the question of whether modest empirical subjectivism is true. We shall then be in a better position to return to the theory of *Verstehen* and to reconstruct the point of view that probably lies behind Abel's argument.

The Synoptic Problem is the problem of explaining why there are certain agreements and disagreements among the texts of the New Testament Gospels of St. Matthew, St. Mark and St. Luke. The agreements and disagreements at issue are legion. In examining them, I shall use the expressions, "St. Matthew," "St. Mark," and so on, to refer respectively to the *authors* of the several gospels—whoever these authors may be—and the expressions, "Matthew," "Mark," and so on, to refer to the *Gospels* themselves.

Some of the more significant of these agreements and disagreements are the following: (1) Most of the subject matter of Mark is also in Matthew, and much of it is also in Luke. There is little of the subject matter of Mark that is not also in either Matthew or Luke. Matthew and Luke, on the other hand, contain much subject matter that is not in Mark. (2) Subject matter that is in all three Gospels usually occurs in the same order. When common subject matter is ordered differently in Matthew than it is in Mark, Luke's order tends to agree with the order in Mark. When it is ordered differently in Luke than it is in Mark, Matthew's order tends to agree with the order of Mark. (3) Matthew and Luke, in the subject matter they share with Mark, are often similar in wording, and Matthew and Luke tend not to have significant words in common unless Mark has them also. Frequently, Mark and Matthew will share the same wording, while Luke diverges, or Mark and Luke will do so, while Matthew diverges.

The agreements and disagreements that need to be explained, as these examples illustrate, are primarily of subject matter, of the order in which subject matter is presented, and of wording. Virtually all New Testament scholars feel that these agreements and disagreements are not coincidental, but are explicable only if there are relationships of literary dependency among these three Gospels. The debate over the Synoptic Problem is the debate over what these relationships of literary dependency are.

The modern discussion of the Synoptic Problem began in the latter half of the eighteenth century in Germany, when scholars such as Lessing, Herder and Eichhorn subjected the traditional account of the relationships among the New Testament Gospels to vigorous criticism.[8] During the next hundred years, scholars proposed literally hundreds of hypotheses to account for these relationships, but no clear consensus emerged. However, with the publication in 1863 of the work of Holtzmann, attention began to be focused on a narrower range of alternatives. The history of the debate subsequent to

1863 is largely the history of the triumph of what came to be called "the two-document hypothesis" and the evolution of that hypothesis into the form in which it received its classic defense in B. H. Streeter's *The Four Gospels*, published in 1924.

Throughout the twentieth century a near consensus of New Testament scholars have felt that the best solution to the Synoptic Problem is the two-document hypothesis. This hypothesis consists of two claims: first, that St. Matthew and St. Luke each used a written version of Mark virtually identical with our own from which they drew much of the subject matter for their own Gospels; secondly, that St. Matthew and St. Luke made large additions to their reproductions of Marcan material, which they drew from a common source (which historians have named "Q"). I shall call the first of these two claims, "the priority of Mark," and the second, "the existence of Q."

The two-document hypothesis is still the dominant view, but since the early 1950s, scholars have argued increasingly for competing solutions to the Synoptic Problem. Some scholars, for instance, have revived the so-called Griesbach hypothesis, according to which St. Matthew wrote first, St. Luke wrote second and used Matthew as a source, St. Mark wrote third and used both Matthew and Luke as sources, and there is no Q. But there is no consensus among recent critics of the two-document hypothesis as to how the Synoptic Problem should be solved.

I want now to consider several examples of kinds of arguments that have played a significant part in the debate over the Synoptic Problem and that are relevant to our consideration of *Verstehen*. For this purpose I am asking you to understand the expression "historical judgment" to mean an assessment, on grounds that are not made explicit, of the relative likelihood of competing historical claims. Numerous examples follow. What makes historical judgments methodologically interesting is not that historians do not confirm them explicitly, but rather that often historians cannot confirm them explicitly. Historians of the Synoptic Problem, for instance, often use arguments that depend on historical judgments even though they cannot confirm those judgments explicitly. Thus, historians often use arguments that depend on judgments that they cannot defend.

The question remains whether historians may use arguments that depend on historical judgments that they cannot defend. In the debate over the Synoptic Problem, proponents of every solution to the Problem use such arguments so routinely, and in such crucial ways, that it is difficult to see how they can effectively reduce their dependence on them without undermining the cases they make for their respective solutions. In other words, historians cannot conduct the debate over the Synoptic Problem as they do or continue it as a viable historical debate in the absence of arguments that depend essentially on historical judgments. I shall explain why by considering three sources of arguments that have figured importantly in the debate over the Synoptic Problem.

Style and the Mode of Composition

Throughout the modern discussion of the Synoptic Problem, scholars have placed great weight on the literary styles in which the Gospels are written. E. A. Abbott, for instance, in an article published in 1879, claims to have "proved by reductio ad absurdum" that St. Mark did not use Matthew and Luke as sources:

> For suppose that he did so copy, it follows that he must not only have constructed a narrative based upon two others, borrowing here a piece from Matthew and here a piece from Luke, but that he must have deliberately determined to insert, and must have adopted his narrative so as to insert, every word that was common to Matthew and Luke. The difficulty of doing this is enormous, and will be patent to anyone who will try to perform a similar feat himself. To embody the whole of even one document in a narrative of one's own, without copying it verbatim, and to do this in a free and natural manner, requires no little care. But to take two documents, to put them side by side and analyze their common matter, then to write a narrative, graphic, abrupt, and in all respects the opposite of artificial, which shall contain every phrase and word that is common to both—this would be a *tour de force*

even for a skillful literary forger of these days, and may be dismissed as an impossibility for the writer of the Second Gospel.[9]

Several influential New Testament scholars accepted Abbott's argument. Their acceptance of it was, in the opinion of one historian of the Synoptic Problem, "one of the most important contributing factors to the eventual consensus that the priority of Mark was firmly established by nineteenth-century criticism."[10]

Streeter, in 1924, also appeals to the style in which Mark is written in order to argue for the priority of Mark:

> The difference between the style of Mark and of the other two is not merely that they both write better Greek. It is the difference which always exists between the spoken and the written language. Mark reads like a shorthand account of a story by an impromptu speaker—with all the repetitions, redundancies, and digressions which are characteristic of living speech . . . Matthew and Luke use the more succinct and carefully chosen language of one who writes and then revises an article for publication.[11]

Finally, G. M. Styler, in a well-known paper published in 1966, claims that "of all the arguments for the priority of Mark, the strongest is that based on the freshness and circumstantial character of his narrative."[12]

There are differences among these arguments. But it is what they have in common that is most important. Each draws attention to a feature of the style in which Mark is written. Each claims, at least implicitly, that it is more likely that St. Mark would have written in that style if he had written first than if he had used either Matthew or Luke as a source. The scholars who use these arguments do not defend this historical judgment.

The Absence of Plausible Motivation

One of the main arguments for the priority of Mark is that St. Mark would have had no plausible motive to write his Gospel as he did had he not written first. Streeter put this point colorfully. In responding to the Augustinian view that

St. Mark was an epitomizer of Matthew, Streeter notes that Matthew is generally more concise than Mark, and that this is hard to explain unless one assumes the priority of Mark:

> Now there is nothing antecedently improbable in the idea that for certain purposes an abbreviated version of the Gospel might be desired; but only a lunatic would leave out Matthew's account of the Infancy, the Sermon on the Mount, and practically all the parables, in order to get room for purely verbal expansion of what was retained. On the other hand, if we suppose Mark to be the older document, the verbal compression and omission of minor detail seen in the parallels in Matthew has an obvious purpose in that it gives more room for the introduction of a mass of highly important teaching material not found in Mark.[13]

The historical judgment underlying this argument is that it is more likely that St. Mark wrote before St. Matthew than that he used Matthew as a source, since had St. Mark used Matthew as a source it is unlikely that he would have been motivated to write his Gospel as he did. Streeter does not defend this historical judgment.

Scholars often support the existence of Q in a similar fashion. Werner Kümmel, for instance, in the 14th edition of his *Introduction to the New Testament*, notes that the existence of Q proceeds from the insight that Matthew and Luke have an extensive amount of common material that neither St. Luke could have taken directly out of Matthew nor St. Matthew directly out of Luke.[14] Kümmel argues that it is "completely untenable" to suppose that St. Luke used Matthew as a source. Part of his reason is this:

> What could have moved Luke to break up Matthew's Sermon on the Mount and to embody part of it in his Sermon on the Plain, to distribute part over the various chapters of his Gospel, and to omit part?[15]

The question is rhetorical. Kümmel's argument depends on the historical judgment that it is more likely that St. Luke did not use Matthew as a source than that he did, since it is unlikely that had St. Luke used Matthew as a source he would have been motivated to break up St. Matthew's version of the Sermon on the Mount in the way described. Kümmel does not defend this historical judgment.

Inappropriate Order or Content and Mode of Composition

Sometimes scholars claim that because the order in which material is presented in a Gospel, or even the material itself, is inappropriate, it is more likely that the Gospel was written using certain sources than that it was written without those sources. Kümmel, for instance, argues on the basis of inappropriate order that St. Luke probably used Mark as a source:

> Luke 4:23 speaks of miracles which took place in Capernaum, about which Luke, however, does not report until 4:31ff., because Mark 6:1ff. is placed before Mark 1:21ff par. Luke 4:31ff. In 4:38ff. Simon is named, whose calling Luke does not relate until 5:1ff. (put in a different place from Mark 1:16ff.).[16]

And Kümmel uses a similar strategy to argue that St. Matthew probably used Mark as a source:

> Both controversy discourses (Mt. 9:9–17) are out of place in the miracle cycle of Matthew and are to be explained only by the fact that these pericopes in Mark followed here.[17]

Kümmel does not defend his historical judgments that the explanations which he prefers of these features of Luke and Matthew are more likely than competing explanations of them.

Styler, on the other hand, argues on the basis of inappropriate content that St. Matthew probably used Mark as a source.

> We have passed on to an argument which to the present writer puts the priority of Mk beyond serious doubt, *viz.* that there are passages where Matt goes astray through misunderstanding, yet betrays a knowledge of the authentic version—the version which is given by Mk. The two accounts of the death of the Baptist (Mk

vi. 17–29, Matt xiv. 3–12) contain clear examples of this. Mk states
fully the attitude of Herod to John; he respected him, but was
perplexed; and it was Herodias who was keen to kill him. And the
story that follows explains how in spite of the king's reluctance she
obtained her desire. Matt, whose version is much briefer, states
that Herod wanted to kill John. But this must be an error; the
story, which perfectly fits Mk's setting, does not fit Matt's introduction; and at xiv. 9 Matt betrays the fact that he really knows the
full version by slipping in the statement that "the king" was sorry.
It is surely clear that Matt, in a desire to abbreviate, has oversim-
plified his introduction.[18]

Styler does not defend his historical judgment that the explanation which he prefers of these differences between Mark
and Matthew is more plausible than competing explanations
of them.

The arguments quoted above, although they differ from each
other in interesting ways, have three things in common. First,
they are no more persuasive than the historical judgments on
which they depend. To whatever extent one does not find the
historical judgments persuasive, to at least that extent one
ought not to find the arguments themselves persuasive. Secondly, the scholars who use these arguments do not defend
the historical judgments on which they depend (nor, so far as
I know, does anyone else). Thirdly, it would be difficult to
argue convincingly, via arguments that do not themselves depend on historical judgments, that the historical judgments
on which these arguments depend ought to be accepted. A
closer look at these arguments reveals why this is so.
    The historical judgments that underlie the three groups of
examples mentioned are roughly these: Arguments in the
first group depend on the historical judgment that it is more
likely that St. Mark would have written his Gospel with the
stylistic features that it has, had he written first, than had he
used either Matthew or Luke as a source. Arguments in the
second group depend on the historical judgment that it is
more likely that St. Mark (or St. Luke) would have been motivated to write his Gospel as he did, had he written his Gospel

without using Matthew as a source, than had he used Matthew as a source. Arguments in the third group depend on the historical judgment that it is more likely that Matthew (or Luke) would include certain inappropriate features that it includes, had St. Matthew (or St. Luke) used Mark as a source, than had he not used Mark as a source.

Consider the historical judgment that underlies arguments in the first group. Of the three, this would seem to be the easiest, by far, to defend without appeal to historical judgment. But how could one defend it? One could to some extent specify those stylistic features of Mark, such as its pleonasms, which are widely regarded as symptomatic of the priority of Mark. But how would one specify properties such as "fresh" and "non-artificial" that have played such an important role in the debate, particularly since it is not just the presence of certain detachable stylistic features, but rather the way in which they are embedded in various specific contexts, that is thought to support the priority of Mark? And the mere specification of general stylistic features of Mark would not thereby avoid dependence on a historical judgment. The only way to avoid such dependence is first, to formulate a generalization that correlates types of stylistic features with types of circumstances under which documents are composed, and secondly, to confirm this generalization by suitable statistical data, and thirdly, to give good reason to think that this generalization is applicable to the times and circumstances under which Mark was composed.

Neither Abbott nor Streeter nor Styler attempt to defend their historical judgment in this or any other manner. So far as I know, no other New Testament scholar attempts to defend it either, in spite of the long and venerable career of the arguments that depend on it. Furthermore, the prospects for defending the historical judgment underlying this first group of arguments were not bright when Abbott wrote and are at best only slightly brighter today. If Abbott (or Streeter, or Styler) had tried to defend the historical judgment underlying his argument in the way sketched, he probably would have failed. Assume for the moment that this is so. If one thinks nevertheless that Abbott and Streeter and Styler may argue as they have—that it is methodologically permissible to draw conclusions from arguments that depend on historical judgments that cannot themselves be defended—then one apparently believes that some historians possess a capacity for assessing on implicit grounds, or intuitively, the relative likelihood of at least some competing historical claims, and that this capacity is more reliable than any other available technique. This is precisely what many *Verstehen*-theorists have maintained.

I could easily extend my discussion of the historical judgments that underlie arguments in the first group of examples to include the even more troublesome historical judgments underlying arguments in the second and third groups of examples. It is instructive to consider, for instance, what generalizations would have to be made explicit and defended in order to defend the arguments based on considerations of inappropriate order and content in ways which eliminate their dependence on historical judgments—say, in order to defend Styler's claim that St. Matthew betrays the fact that he really knows St. Mark's version of the death of John the Baptist since he slips in the statement that the king was sorry. I leave this task to the reader.

One might object to my assumption that if Abbott or Streeter or Styler had tried to defend the historical judgment underlying his argument in ways which eliminate his dependence on a historical judgment, he would have failed. The only way to prove that this historical judgment cannot be defended would be to make an appropriate attempt to defend it and fail. So far as I know, no one has ever tried to defend it, a fact that is significant. Remember, though, that the case for the two-document hypothesis, as well as the cases for competing solutions to the Synoptic Problem, do not gather their strength from just a handful of arguments that individually or collectively are thought to be decisive. They depend rather upon literally hundreds of detailed textual interpretations, almost all of which depend on historical judgments. These arguments provide relatively strong support for a particular solution to the Synoptic Problem, if they do, only in a cumulative fashion. Thus, nothing that is significant hinges on my being right in thinking that each of the specific arguments mentioned above or that figures importantly in the debate over the Synoptic Problem depends essentially on a historical judgment. In the debate over the Synoptic Problem, arguments that depend on historical judgments are as plentiful as blackberries. Even if the historical judgments that underlie some of these arguments can be defended in ways which eliminate dependence on a historical judgment, it is doubtful that many can be so defended. This too might be questioned. But I shall assume it in what follows. The question, then, is whether historians may use arguments that depend essentially on historical judgments.

There are two main ways to try to show that historians ought not to use arguments that depend essentially on historical judgments. First, some say that one problem with arguments that depend essentially on historical judgments is that historians invariably judge differently. This is said to be significant because there is no reason why anyone, including the historians involved, should prefer the judgment of one historian to the conflicting judgment of another comparably qualified historian. Thus, arguments that depend essentially on historical judgments are said to be useless.

The problem with this objection is simply that historians do often agree on historical judgments. The history of the debate over the Synoptic Problem shows that such agreement can be widespread and durable.

Secondly, some suggest that those who use arguments that depend essentially on historical judgments need what I shall call a "reliability argument," that is, good reason for thinking that agreement among historians on a historical judgment is a reliable indication of its truth. It is possible that such agreement is unrelated to data that, if made explicit, would confirm the judgment. One who simply assumes that agreement on historical judgments is a reliable guide to the truth does so on faith. And faith of this sort has no place in genuine science, or, by implication, in any historiography that is done as reliably as possible.

This sort of consideration seems to be what lies behind
Abel's objection to the use of *Verstehen* as a technique of
confirmation. The problem with this objection is in its assumption that a reliability argument is needed. The objection
ignores the fact that all of us routinely use arguments that
depend essentially on historical judgments for practical purposes—in business, in government, in courts of law, and in the
private conduct of our lives—as if they were a reliable guide
to truth, or at least as reliable as any available alternative. We
use them in all of these contexts to make decisions, sometimes
decisions of great moment for humankind, some of which we
regard as paradigmatic of responsible decisions. We would
not use them to the extent we do, or regard them as compatible with responsible decision making, unless we regarded
them as a relatively reliable guide to the truth.

No responsible person would suggest that we ought not to
employ arguments that depend essentially on historical judgments for practical purposes. Why then insist that we ought
not to use them in historical studies? Those who do so insist
owe us what I shall call an "austerity argument": either good
reason why arguments that depend essentially on historical
judgments ought not to be used for practical purposes; or an
account of how their responsible use for practical purposes
differs from their use in historical studies; or a justification
for insisting on greater austerity in historical studies than in
the practical affairs of life.

It may seem that an austerity argument could be provided.
There are good reasons, it is sometimes said, for insisting on
greater austerity in historical studies than in the practical
affairs of life. For one thing, there is less urgency to arrive
at a decision in historical studies. In practical affairs, unlike
historical studies, often we must decide in order to act. When
the enemy is at our door, we must act promptly or else we
may perish. When an accused killer is in the dock, we must
judge his guilt or innocence promptly or else justice will be
thwarted. But there is no comparable urgency in historical
studies.[19]

One problem with this austerity argument is that it assumes
there is no urgency to solving the problems of historical studies. No urgency for whom? Many scholars have regarded

solving the Synoptic Problem as a prerequisite to determining what is most reasonable to believe about what Jesus did and said. For some this has been an urgent matter. For others it is urgent to understand how the holocaust could have happened, or why racial prejudice has been so virulent in the United States, or what the founding fathers of the United States intended by enacting the Constitution and the Bill of Rights. Another problem is that practical decisions made on the basis of arguments that depend on historical judgments may be responsibly made even when there is no urgency to act. I may infer responsibly from a friend's cryptic note where he probably left the novel he promised me, even though it is not urgent that I act on my inference.

Some suggest another reason for greater austerity in historical studies: the proper objective of historical studies is, or at least should be, to arrive at scientific knowledge.[20] In practical affairs our objective is not this but something else, ordinarily to arrive at responsible action. And a proposition counts as an item of scientific knowledge only if it is confirmed by data, all of which are publicly accessible. The conclusions of arguments that depend essentially on historical judgments are not confirmed exclusively by such data. Hence, one cannot arrive at scientific knowledge or promote the proper objective of historical studies by arguments that depend essentially on historical judgments.

This austerity argument is inconclusive. How do we know that the ultimate objective of historical studies is to arrive at knowledge which is confirmed by publically accessible data? Perhaps the best or the most reliable historiography would be "unscientific" in this respect. But even if we allow that the ultimate objective of historical studies is to arrive at knowledge that is confirmed by publicly accessible data, what may historians do when this objective is unattainable? Typically this ultimate objective is unattainable, at least if the problems to be solved are the problems that historians usually address.

Although it is not necessary to provide a reliability argument in order to defend the use by historians of historical judgments, a weak reliability argument may be provided. We could have good reason for thinking that someone's historical judgment was reliable, even though no adequate grounds for that judgment could be given. For instance, a historian's ability to discover the truth by means of arguments that depend essentially on historical judgments could be established by repeated, independent verification of her conclusions to the point where we are entitled to say on inductive grounds and without independent verification that her judgment in a new case is probably true.[21]

Do we ever have this sort of verification? Yes. A good historian's ability to make reliable historical judgments is repeatedly tested. Admittedly, these tests are informal, but informal tests are still tests. Historical judgments are routinely made for practical purposes, and often we subsequently discover whether inferences based on those judgments are true. Recall the example about interpreting my friend's cryptic note. The testing of a trained historian goes far beyond the routine testing of everyday life. In the professional training of a historian and in the dialogue characteristic of historical controversy, there are numerous opportunities to check one's historical judgments against the judgments of others and against the truth. For instance, in the early stages of the examination of a large body of related documents, it is natural to continually form tacit hypotheses based on historical judgments about what sorts of things the documents yet to be examined will contain. Then when one examines the documents one checks one's judgments against the truth. So far as checking one's historical judgments against those of others is concerned, remember that the ability to make reliable historical judgments is central to traditional historical methodology. Isaiah Berlin put this reminder nicely: "A man who lacks common intelligence can be a physicist of genius, but not even a mediocre historian."[22] Consider, too, how often the work of a well-regarded historian has been favorably evaluated by other trained historians in the course of his professional preparation and during his rise from obscurity to relative prominence.

Suppose that such a historian is favorably placed to make a particular historical judgment, and that a preponderance of other comparably qualified and comparably placed historians agree with his judgment. Suppose also that you and I, as informed and intelligent readers, also agree with his judgment. Surely then we have some reason to think that his judgment is reliable. Enough reason? How can we settle the question of how high we should set our standards? Perhaps we should simply remember that in the absence of an austerity argument we have a sound basis for concluding that historians may often use arguments that depend on historical judgments even though no explicit defense of these judgments can be given. The reliability argument sketched above, albeit impressionistic, provides some justification for using such arguments. And in the absence of an austerity argument, there is no reason not to use them.

It may be tempting to object that the lack of a stronger reliability argument is itself a good reason not to use arguments that depend on historical judgments. But this objection would prove too much. The absence of a stronger reliability argument, then, would also be a good reason not to use historical judgments for practical purposes. But that would be absurd. We cannot shed our conception of the past with no alternative conception with which to replace it. And we cannot justify an alternative conception without appeal to arguments that depend on historical judgments. In the end, the justification for using arguments that depend on historical judgments, whether for practical purposes or in historical studies, is the absence of a comparably reliable alternative. Whatever their defects, arguments that depend on historical judgments are often the best arguments we have.

A case might be made that although there is no blanket methodological objection to the use of arguments that depend essentially on historical judgments, the results of such arguments should be regarded as less reliable than the results of arguments that depend on "more scientific" procedures. All else being equal, this may be true. The trouble is that in real life, all else rarely is equal. We not only do but often must rely, in important ways, on arguments that depend on historical judgments. Since this is so, it makes sense to acknowledge openly the critical role of historical judgments in our lives and to learn, if we can, how to make them more reliably.

There are two additional issues worth mentioning. First, even if historians may *sometimes* use arguments that depend essentially on historical judgments, it does not follow that they may *often* use them. The debate over the Synoptic Problem, it might be said, drawn as it is from so-called literary history, is surely a special case. Even if historians of that debate may rely heavily upon arguments that depend on historical judgments, how often may historians in more conventional debates rely upon them?

There is no denying that the debate over the Synoptic Problem is useful for the argument developed in this chapter. That is why it was chosen. But the differences between this debate and other more conventional historical debates are more differences of degree than differences of kind. Problems of interpreting literary texts—official documents, court decisions, records of speeches, letters, diaries, and so on—figure importantly in many significant historical debates and often involve problems of historical judgment that raise the same philosophical issues as those we saw in the debate over the Synoptic Problem.[23] In addition, it is not just the interpretation of literary texts that motivates arguments that depend on historical judgments, but also the consideration of individual and collective activity of a wide variety of kinds. Skeptics need only consult their favorite historical texts.

The second point is that my conclusion is relevant, at least if one accepts two assumptions, to the question of whether history is subjective. The assumptions are that historians rely to a greater degree than do scientists on judgments that cannot be defended, and that this difference between the ways in which historians and scientists characteristically argue cannot soon change.

These assumptions are plausible. Consider once again the arguments used as examples from the debate over the Synoptic Problem. Each argument depends on a historical judgment that is not, and, it seems, cannot be defended. In each case, the only thing that would suffice as a defense, aside from inductive grounds for confidence in the historian who makes the judgment, is a good generalization or theory. For each of these examples, then, historical judgments are being used as a surrogate for appeal to well confirmed generalizations or theories. This is typical of the use by historians of historical judgments. Although scientists also rely on analogous forms of judgment, it would seem that historians routinely rely on historical judgments in contexts where scientists would more often appeal to generalizations or theories. Compare, for example, historical studies proper with historical sciences such as geology and astronomy. Since suitable generalizations or theories are hard to discover, it seems that this difference between the ways in which historians and scientists defend their claims will not soon change.

The point is not that historians typically have less evidence than do scientists to back up their claims. Lack of evidence, in and of itself, is no barrier to objectivity, since one need claim no more on behalf of his views than he is entitled to claim on the basis of whatever evidence is available. As we saw in our discussion of explanation, for instance, historians need claim no more on behalf of the interpretations they favor than that these interpretations are better supported by the available evidence than are competing interpretations. The point is that historians, more than scientists, must rely upon judgments that they cannot defend in order even to determine which of several competing claims are better supported by the available evidence. Thus, historians, more than scientists, must rely upon judgments that they cannot defend in order to support the main sorts of claims that are characteristic of their discipline.

Surely one significant measure of the objectivity of a discipline is the degree to which its practitioners must rely upon judgments that they cannot defend in order to support the main sorts of claims that are characteristic of their discipline. The more they must rely upon such judgments, all else being equal, the more subjective their discipline. The comparisons between historical studies and science mentioned above, if acceptable, are a reason for claiming that historical studies are more subjective than science. The comparisons mentioned do not *establish* that historical studies are more subjective than science, for there may be different, countervailing respects in which science is more subjective. And the comparisons are not a reason for claiming that historical studies are *in principle* more subjective than science. I am not arguing for conceptual subjectivism, but at most for modest empirical subjectivism. Nevertheless, the comparisons mentioned are *a* reason for claiming that historical studies are *intractably* more subjective than science, that is, that historical studies are in fact more subjective in ways that cannot easily or soon be changed. In sum, in historical studies, more so, it seems, than in science, there really is no substitute for the brewmaster's nose.

APPENDIX: HISTORICAL
COUNTEREXAMPLES

THE CENTRAL claim of the positivist analysis of historical explanation is that historical explanations of particular events and facts are true only if corresponding general causal laws are true. This claim is restricted to those historical explanations that are causal and that are sufficient, or nearly sufficient, for what they explain.

In the debate over historical explanation, proponents and critics alike thought this central claim has implications for how historians should do history. Most thought this central claim implies that historians can properly defend their causal explanations of particular events and facts only if they can also defend corresponding general causal laws. But historians rarely defend their explanations by defending corresponding general causal laws. Therefore, proponents of the positivist analysis argued that historians should change their ways while opponents argued that because it is usually inappropriate for historians to try to back up their explanations with causal generalizations, the positivist analysis must be false.

The debate focused on the positivist analysis itself rather than on the actual dynamics of historical controversy. To the extent that historical controversy was examined, proponents and critics, both under the spell of the positivist analysis, tended to look only at the ways historians argue directly for the explanations they propose. No one paid much attention to the ways historians argue indirectly for their explanations by arguing against the explanations they oppose or seek to supplement. Thus, no one realized that historians routinely support their explanations with a kind of indirect argument—a "historical counterexample"—that itself suggests that the central claim of the positivist analysis is correct.[1]

I argued in Chapter 2 that the positivist analysis does not imply that historians should attempt to back up their explanations with covering generalizations. Why, then, bother now with the question of whether historical counterexamples support the positivist analysis? There are several reasons. First, to help answer the question of how historical counterexamples—a commonplace of historical argumentation with obvious prima facie relevance to the debate over the positivist analysis—could have been overlooked in the more than thirty-year-long debate over historical explanation. My answer: because the debate over the positivist analysis drew attention away from the examination of actual historical argumentation. Secondly, to help answer the question of why humanists, despite decades of persistent efforts, were never able to formulate an argument that was widely regarded, even among themselves, as having refuted the central claim of the positivist analysis. My answer: because the central claim of the positivist analysis is true. Thirdly, to reinforce the point that my criticisms of positivists in Chapter 2 and elsewhere should be understood not as criticisms of the positivist analysis, but rather as criticisms of assumptions that underlay the debate and were shared both by positivists and humanists. And finally, to introduce the examination of historical counterexamples in their own right. Although the use of historical counterexamples is a prominent and important way in which historians support their explanations, historians often present them unclearly and thus generate needless debate of their own. My examination will suggest ways in which historians can formulate historical counterexamples more clearly.

Historical counterexamples are arguments with one premise, which asserts that some event occurred or fact obtained that was not accompanied by another event or fact of a specified kind, and a conclusion, which asserts that some event or fact similar to the former was not a sufficient cause of some event or fact similar to the latter.[2] I have argued that although historians are rarely able to show, and seldom attempt to show, that the causal explanations they *propose* express *sufficient* causes of what they explain, they often use historical counterexamples to show that the causal explanations they *oppose*, or seek to supplement, express *insufficient* causes of what they explain.

Each of the following quotations suggests at least one historical counterexample:

> Depopulation, the Christian religion, the fiscal system have all been assigned as causes of the Empire's decline in strength. If these or any of them were responsible for its dismemberment by the barbarians in the West, it may be asked how it was that in the East, where the same causes operated, the Empire survived much longer intact and united.
>
> J. B. Bury, 1958, 1:308–309.

> If the frontier alone was a self-sufficient source of democracy and individualism, whatever the institutions and ideas the frontiersmen brought with them, frontiers elsewhere ought to have had a similar effect. The early frontier of French Canada, the South American frontier, and the Siberian frontier should have fostered democracy and individualism.
>
> Richard Hofstadter, 1966, 102.

> Sometimes on a coast where the hinterland was sparsely populated, like North Africa, a port, with its indispensable source of water, might exist as a meeting point for boats and fishermen, without a town having grown up around it: proof, if it were needed, that the functions of a port are not sufficient to create a town.
>
> Fernand Braudel, 1972, 1:108.

> The [Court/Country] antithesis is only one version of the normal state of tension that exists in all organized societies between the centralizing and the decentralizing forces: between Hamilton and Jefferson, for example. Since the polarity continued to play an important political role in England at least for another seventy-five years after 1640, it cannot be regarded as the exclusive cause for a breakdown of government.
>
> Lawrence Stone, 1972, 108.

> What types of evidence are necessary to establish with reasonable certainty a 'social interpretation' of the rise of abolitionism before 1840? Clearly, one type of necessary evidence is that . . . individual

abolitionists . . . possessed the specified social background. But would it not be desirable or perhaps necessary to present a second type of evidence, evidence showing by comparison that other individuals did *not* have the same social background as the abolitionists? For if non-abolitionists (in proportionate numbers) came from social backgrounds identical to the backgrounds of the abolitionists . . . the social background could not logically be *the determining* factor in the rise of abolitionism before 1840. . . .

Robert A. Skotheim, 1973, 50.

Bury's remarks imply a historical counterexample since they imply, in context, that neither "depopulation," nor "the Christian religion," nor "the fiscal system," nor all of these jointly was a sufficient cause of the Western Empire's decline in strength. Hofstadter's remarks imply a historical counterexample since they imply, in context, that "the frontier alone" was not a sufficient cause of democracy and individualism in the United States. And so on. One could multiply examples from historical studies at great length.[3]

Historians use historical counterexamples to show that because a corresponding general causal law is *not* true, then some event(s) or fact(s) was *not* a sufficient cause of another. I shall assume for the time being that the causal law in question is a universal law, rather than merely a probabilistic law. Later, I shall explain why this simplifying assumption is innocuous.

Anyone who considers the examples quoted will recognize that historical counterexamples are an exceedingly common and respectable form of argument in historical studies and that prima facie they are valid. He or she will also recognize that prima facie their validity constitutes a powerful argument for the central claim of the positivist analysis. The connection between historical counterexamples and the positivist analysis is not esoteric. It is obvious. A particular causal explanation is inferred to be insufficient because the corresponding general causal law is false. Thus, the fact that historical counterexamples were all but ignored in the over thirty-year-long debate over the positivist theory of historical explanation is itself historically significant, a point to which I shall return below. For now, I want to consider the question of whether historical counterexamples are actually valid arguments.

Objection 1. Historical counterexamples are invalid since the events designated in their premises may not be similar in all relevant respects to the events designated in their conclusions. Consider, for instance, the following argument:

> (A) (1) There was a flood which was unaccompanied by famine.
> So, (2) *this* flood was not a sufficient cause of *this* famine.

(A) is a typical historical counterexample. Historical counterexamples infer from the premise that a certain kind of event has not always been accompanied by a certain kind of result the conclusion that a specific event of the former kind was not sufficient for a specific result of the latter kind. The conclusion does not follow. In (A) the flood or floods in virtue of which the premise is true may not be similar in all causally relevant respects to the flood referred to in the conclusion. For example, the flood referred to in the conclusion, but not the other floods, may have inundated crops essential to feeding a population. Thus, even though the other floods were not sufficient for famines, still the one referred to in the conclusion may have been sufficient for a famine.

Reply. It is true, for the reasons given, that arguments like (A) are not valid. Hence, if historical counterexamples are arguments like (A), they are not valid either. But most historical counterexamples are not like (A). Rather they are arguments like:

> (B) (1) There was a flood that was unaccompanied by a famine.
> So, (3) the mere fact that there was a flood was not a sufficient cause of the fact that there was a famine.

(A) and (B) have the same premise, but different conclusions. The conclusion of (A) is that one particular event was not sufficient for another. The conclusion of (B) is that *the mere fact that* there was a particular event of a certain kind—a flood—was not sufficient for the fact that there was a particular event of another kind—a famine. (A)'s conclusion—(2)—is stronger than (B)'s conclusion—(3). Hence, even though (1) does not imply (2), it may still imply the weaker conclusion, (3).

The objection to (A) was that the flood or floods in virtue of which premise (1) is true may not be similar in all relevant respects to the flood referred to in conclusion (2), and hence that even though those floods were not sufficient for famines, this one may be. That objection is irrelevant to (B). Whatever other properties the floods in virtue of which premise (1) is true may have had, they were still floods unaccompanied by a famine. And all that (B) concludes is that *the mere fact that* something is a flood cannot be a sufficient cause of a famine. In other words, (B) allows that a flood could be sufficient for a famine, but denies that a flood, *merely in virtue of being a flood* and quite apart from whatever other properties it might have had, could be sufficient for a famine. The proof—premise (1)—is that some floods do not cause famines. Surely (B) is valid.

Many historians formulate their historical counterexamples in ways which suggest that they are drawing a conclusion like (2). Bury, for instance, in the remarks quoted, appears to be drawing the conclusion that the depopulation in the Western Empire was not sufficient for the Western Empire's decline in strength. Nevertheless, there is a natural and charitable interpretation of most historical counterexamples that appear in serious historical studies according to which their conclusions are like (3) rather than (2). For instance, Bury may be understood to conclude only that the mere fact that there was a depopulation in the Western Empire, or the mere fact that there was a depopulation with such and such characteristics in the Western Empire, characteristics that the depopulation in the Eastern Empire shared, was not sufficient for the fact that the Western Empire declined in strength. Historical counterexamples whose conclusion is like (3) are not vulnerable to Objection 1.

While Objection 1 does not cut deeply as an objection to the use of historical counterexamples in historical studies, it does draw attention to a problem with the way many historical counterexamples are presented. For one thing, it is often unclear whether the conclusion of a historical counterexample is like (2) or like (3). For another, if a historical counterexample is interpreted charitably as an argument whose conclusion is like (3), it is often unclear which facts are expressed by the premise and conclusion. For instance, when Bury speaks of the "same causes" operating in the Western and the Eastern Empires, which causes exactly does he mean? Christianity, say, spread in both Empires, but not in exactly the same way or with exactly the same characteristics and consequences. Do Bury's remarks refer to all of those events which collectively constitute the spread of Christianity in the Western and the Eastern Empires, or to the mere fact that Christianity spread in both the Western and the Eastern Empires, or to the different fact that Christianity spread in such and such a manner in both the Western and the Eastern Empires? My guess is the latter, but then it is not clear how Bury would flesh out the "such and such." There is a similar ambiguity in Bury's comments on "depopulation" and "the fiscal system," and a similar ambiguity in the quoted remarks of Hofstadter, Braudel and Stone. Objection 1 draws attention to the fact that such ambiguity breeds confusion. The Reply suggests a way to avoid that kind of ambiguity and its attendant confusion.

Objection 2. Let us call historical counterexamples like (B) "basic historical counterexamples," and grant, for the sake of argument, that they are valid.[4] It does not follow, and is not true, that *most* historical counterexamples that appear in serious historical studies are basic historical counterexamples. Most are not, and they differ from basic historical counterexamples in ways which undermine their validity. In basic historical counterexamples, the fact expressed in the premise involves the same properties, say, the property of being a flood, as the fact expressed in the conclusion. In most historical counterexamples, the fact expressed in the premise has specified spatial and/or temporal properties different from the fact expressed in the conclusion.

Consider Bury's remarks once again. One of the historical counterexamples he expressed may be rendered as follows:

(C) (4) There was an event that was a depopulation in the Eastern Empire which was not accompanied by an event that was a governmental decline in the Eastern Empire.

So, (5) the fact that there was an event that was a depopulation in the Western Empire was not a sufficient cause of the fact that there was an event that was a governmental decline in the Western Empire.

The fact expressed in the premise, (4), concerns events in the *Eastern* Empire. The fact expressed in the conclusion, (5), concerns events in the *Western* Empire. These two facts are disanalogous with respect to specified spatial location. Thus, (C) is not a basic historical counterexample.

Even if basic historical counterexamples are valid, historical counterexamples like (C) are not valid. The problem with arguments like (C) is similar to the problem with arguments like (A). Arguments like (C) fail to guarantee that the fact expressed in the conclusion is relevantly similar to the corresponding fact expressed in the premise.

Consider the following example: Let F_1 be the fact that there is, at some place, p_1, a combustible material that is raised above its kindling temperature; R_1 the result that there is, at p_1, a fire; and F_2 the fact that there is, at some different place, p_2, a combustible material that is raised above its kindling temperature. Suppose that at p_2 there is no fire. Does it follow that F_1 was not a sufficient cause of R_1? Surely not. F_1 and F_2 are in different places. Thus, they necessarily stand in some different relationships to some other things and events. Because of these different relationships, F_1 could have been sufficient for R_1 even though F_2 was not sufficient for any fact similar to R_1. For instance, suppose there is always at p_1, but never at p_2, oxygen ample for a fire. It follows that F_1 has a relationship to oxygen that F_2 lacks, and because it does, F_1 could have been sufficient for a fire at p_1, even though, in spite of F_2, there was no fire at p_2.

The general moral is that spatial disanalogies between the fact expressed in the premise of a historical counterexample and the corresponding fact expressed in its conclusion may undermine the validity of the argument. Just as there may be causally relevant differences between different particular events, so also there may be causally relevant differences between facts which have different spatial locations. Thus, the problem with arguments like (C) is basically the same as the problem with arguments like (A). In response to (A), we noted that the flood mentioned in conclusion (2) may have had a spatial relationship to crops essential to feeding a population that distinguished it causally from any flood that was unaccompanied by a famine. It is such possibilities which undermine the validity of (A). By the same token, F_1 may have had a causally relevant relationship to oxygen which F_2 lacked. In Bury's argument, (C), a depopulation in the Western Empire necessarily has relationships to many events that a depopulation in the Eastern Empire lacks, and the premise of (C), (4), provides insufficient reason for dismissing such relationships as causally irrelevant. Hence, arguments like (C) are not valid.[5]

Analogous considerations apply to differences of temporal properties. One of Stone's arguments in the remarks quoted above may be rendered as follows:

(D) (6) There was a Court/Country antithesis in England after 1660 which was unaccompanied by a breakdown in government in England after 1660.

So, (7) the fact that there was a Court/Country antithesis in England prior to 1640 was not a sufficient cause of the fact that there was a breakdown in government in England in 1640.

(D) is not valid for the same reason that (C) is not valid, except that in (D) the troublesome properties are temporal, whereas in (C) they are spatial. A fact at one time will necessarily have relationships to other things and events that distinguish it from any fact at some different time. The political situation in England after 1660 was different from the political situation in England prior to 1640. Hence, the fact expressed in (6) had different relationships to some things and events than the fact expressed in (7). Hence, historical counterexamples like (D) are not valid.

Most historical counterexamples that conclude that one fact was not sufficient for another are defective in the same respects in which (C) and (D) are defective, that is, the fact expressed in the premises of such arguments are disanalogous with the corresponding fact expressed in the conclusion either with respect to specified spatial locations or specified temporal locations or both. Hence, most historical counterexamples are not valid.

Reply. Neither the argument attributed to Bury nor the argument attributed to Stone are basic historical counterexamples. It is also true, assuming it makes sense to assign spatial and temporal locations to facts, that the arguments of Bury and Stone infer from a premise that expresses facts with certain spatial and/or temporal locations a conclusion that expresses facts with different spatial and/or temporal locations. However, it has not been shown that the arguments of Bury and Stone, and formally similar arguments, are thereby invalid.

Objection 2 relies on the following claim:

(8) Because F_1 and F_2 have different relationships to other events, F_1 could have been a sufficient cause of R_1 even though F_2 was not a sufficient cause of any fact similar to R_1.

No argument is given for (8). The example used to illustrate it suggests that the proper way to assess the causal sufficiency of a fact is to hold fixed the relationships between it and all other events which occurred on the occasion when it obtained. Thus, we are to assess the causal sufficiency of F_1 and F_2, given that there was at p_1, but not at p_2, "a supply of oxygen ample for a fire." This suggests that we should accept (8) because we should accept some such claim as:

(9) One fact, F, is a sufficient cause of another fact, R, if and only if there is some set of facts that obtained when F obtained, such that F together with the members of that set is a sufficient cause of R.

Claim (9) is unacceptable since it does not insure that F is even a partial cause of R. What follows the "if and only if" in (9) leaves open the possibility that F is simply a redundant addition to a set of facts the members of which, independently of F, are sufficient for R.

It may seem that this problem with (9) can easily be removed by replacing (9) with:

> (10) F is a sufficient cause of R if and only if F is at least a partial cause of R and there is some set of facts that obtained when F obtained, such that F together with the members of that set is a sufficient cause of R.

But, although (10) is not vulnerable to the same problem that defeated (9), it is vulnerable to another. Claim (10) destroys the distinction between partial and sufficient causes. It is a consequence of (10) that any fact that is at least a partial cause of a fact that has a sufficient cause is thereby a sufficient cause of that fact. This consequence is seriously counterintuitive, surely too high a price to pay merely to salvage (8). And there seems no better way to defend (8). One cannot properly assess the causal sufficiency of a fact by holding fixed the relationships between it and all other events that occurred on the occasion when it obtained. Hence, Objection 2 must be rejected.

Although Objection 2 cannot be sustained, it should not be dismissed hastily. It focuses on a serious difficulty concerning our understanding of historical counterexamples. The arguments of Bury and Stone differ from basic historical counterexamples in that there are disanalogies between the facts expressed in the premises of their arguments and the corresponding facts expressed in the conclusions. It appears that such disanalogies do not undermine their validity. However, other disanalogies between the facts expressed in the premises and corresponding facts expressed in the conclusions of historical counterexamples surely do undermine their validity. Objection 2 reminds us that we have no acceptable general criterion for distinguishing between these different sorts of disanalogies.

There is good reason to conclude that all basic and some non-basic historical counterexamples are valid arguments. The most plausible objections to them are unconvincing. And the supposition that they are valid provides a rationale for an important and well-entrenched aspect of historical methodology. But if basic historical counterexamples are valid, how do we explain their validity?

Basic historical counterexamples have the following form:

(BHC) (11) There was an event that was α which was unaccompanied by an event that was β.

So, (12) the mere fact that there was an α was not a sufficient cause of the fact that there was a β.[6]

The Greek letters, α and β, are placeholders for terms that stand for properties (or kinds) of events. Argument (B), our main example of a basic historical counterexample, is an instance of the argument form (BHC).

If (BHC) is a valid argument form, it remains to explain why it is. The only plausible explanation is that the following claim is true:

(13) The fact that there was an α was a sufficient cause of the fact that there was a β only if whenever there is an event that is α, it is accompanied by an event that is β.

Claim (13) is just a version of the central thesis of the positivist analysis of historical explanation. So, if basic historical counterexamples are valid, and (13) is the only plausible explanation of their validity, then the central claim of the positivist analysis of historical explanation is probably true.

The reason (13) is the only plausible explanation of the validity of arguments of form (BHC) is that the premise of a basic historical counterexample,

(11) there was an event that was an α which was unaccompanied by an event that was a β,

has to be incompatible with the antecedent of (13),

(13.1) the mere fact that there was an α was a sufficient cause of the fact that there was a β,

in order to guarantee conclusion (12). But if (11) is incompatible with (13.1), then (13) is true.

Claim (13) is just one way of expressing the central claim of the positivist analysis of historical explanation—namely, that particular causal explanations are true only if their corresponding general causal laws are true—when that claim is applied just to basic historical counterexamples. Thus, (13) provides strong support for the central claim of the positivist analysis. The explanations of other valid forms of historical counterexamples, if we wanted to work them out, would probably collectively provide even stronger support.

Those who object to using (13) to explain the validity of basic historical counterexamples have two alternatives. One is to deny the validity of basic historical counterexamples. But such a denial is hollow unless accompanied by a good objection to their validity. I have examined above what seems to be the most plausible objection and found that it cannot be sustained. In addition, denying the validity of basic historical counterexamples would fly in the face of current historical practice. Basic historical counterexamples are the most plausible of historical counterexamples, which are a common and important aspect of historical methodology. Historical counterexamples are the principal arguments used to establish the negative point that one or more facts were not a sufficient cause of another fact. They are often a crucial element in an argumentative strategy designed to support the positive point that some favored explanation is better than competing explanations. In short, if basic historical counterexamples are not valid arguments, then there is something radically wrong with an important aspect of historical methodology.

The second alternative is to offer a different explanation of the validity of basic historical counterexamples. But it is difficult for me to imagine what such an explanation might be. And in the absence of such an explanation, the claim that causal explanations of particular facts and events are true only if corresponding general causal laws are true receives strong support from an examination of historical methodology.

Note that nothing essential changes if we were to imagine that historical counterexamples are directed against probabilistic, rather than strictly universal, laws. The problem, then, is to explain why historical counterexamples are good inductive arguments rather than valid deductive arguments. But the explanation—that historical counterexamples are good inductive arguments only if particular causal explanations imply the existence of at least probabilistic corresponding general causal laws—remains the same.

Historical counterexamples are not a rare or subtle feature of historical argumentation. Anyone who examines the way historians argue indirectly for their explanations will find that historical counterexamples are a ubiquitous and obvious feature. It is also not difficult to see their relevance to the positivist analysis. How then could so many philosophers and historians have spent so much energy on historical explanation and still not have noticed historical counterexamples? There are, I think, two reasons. The first has already been mentioned: most of the energy spent on historical explanation was spent on the positivist analysis, not on the examination of actual historical argumentation. The other reason is that the positivist theory encourages a non-comparative approach to the question of how historians should defend their explanations, that is, it encourages one to look only at the ways historians argue directly for their explanations. Since both positivists and humanists were under the spell of the positivist theory, the debate raged for decades without anyone seriously considering the ways in which historians argue indirectly for their explanations and the possible relevance to positivist theory of their arguing in these ways.

NOTES

PREFACE

1. The books by Gorman, 1982, and McCullagh, 1984, are obvious examples of important recent work.

2. See especially Hayden White, 1973 and 1984, and Mink, 1978. Canary and Kozicki, 1978 contains several essays and a useful bibliography of the work, to 1977, on narrative form. And Vann, 1987 provides an interesting account of the evolution of Mink's views.

3. Others have occasionally criticized analytic philosophy of history on similar grounds. Compare, for instance, Abraham Kaplan: "There is need in the philosophy of history for more than an understanding of what is true 'in principle' about the writing of history. We need to understand what in fact historians do. In principle, the description, interpretation and explanation of what happened in history may be no different from what applies to any other sort of happenings; in practice there are many special problems. It is absurd to proclaim conclusions about what is true 'in the last analysis,' while we are still floundering in the first analysis" (Kaplan, 1978, p. 28); and also Donald Davidson: "It seems to me that analytic philosophers often exaggerate the value, to workers in a certain area, of giving an analysis of the concepts those workers use. Such analysis is often interesting, but mainly to philosophers" (Davidson, 1978, p. 235).

4. Dray, 1964 and 1966 contain useful select bibliographies of important work. Relatively complete bibliographies are published periodically in *History and Theory*.

1: TWO APPROACHES TO PHILOSOPHY OF HISTORY

1. M. White, 1965, pp. 1–2.

2. I discuss explanation in Chapters 2–4, then objectivity in Chapters 5 and 6. The reason for reversing the order in which these topics were debated historically is that explanation is the more basic topic. What one should say about the prospects for objectivity in historical studies depends more on one's account of explanation than vice versa.

3. For an extended discussion of this example and an elementary account of the "semantic conception of scientific theories" on which it is based, see Giere, 1979, pp. 96–113.

4. The tension between what we would now call scientific and humanistic approaches to the study of human behavior was evident as early as Plato's *Phaedo*, 98b–99d, and it has been with us ever since. It is not likely to go away soon.

2: POSITIVISM AND ITS CRITICS

1. Geyl, 1956, p. 47.

2. M. White, 1965, pp. 22–23. Note that I am not saying White attributes to Geyl the view that Geyl has strong or conclusive evidence for his explanation. Whether someone claims his explanation is partial or sufficient is independent of the question of how much evidence he claims to have for that explanation. One can have strong evidence for the claim that an explanation is at least partial, but only weak evidence for the claim that it is sufficient.

3. M. White, 1965, p. 27.

4. M. White, 1965, pp. 27–28.

5. Murphey, 1973, pp. 89–90, emphasis added.

6. Murphey, 1973, p. 91. See also the remarks of Ernest Nagel quoted toward the beginning of Chapter 4.

7. Hereafter, in discussing (1), I shall ignore the qualification, "or generalizations . . . ," since it is irrelevant to the points I want to make.

8. This remark concerns mainstream historical work. It is not true of certain sub-divisions of historical studies, such as the so-called New Economic History.

3: EXPLANATORY COMPETITION

1. When philosophers have examined actual explanatory competition in historical studies, they have tended to do it through the lens of the positivist theory and primarily in order to ferret out covert generalizations lurking behind seemingly innocent historical explanations. Murphey's analysis of alternative interpretations of Bacon's Rebellion is a good case in point. See Murphey, 1973, pp. 102–112. See also Donagan, 1969, pp. 58–89.

2. Sanders, 1973, p. 361.

3. Items (1.1)–(1.2): Morley and Brainerd, 1956, p. 69; MacKie, 1961, pp. 216–224; Adams, 1973a, p. 27.

4. Adams, 1973a, p. 27.

5. Items (1.3)–(1.5): Morley and Brainerd, 1956, p. 69; Cowgill, 1964, p. 152; Adams, 1973, p. 27.

6. In forest swidden maize agriculture the forest is cleared with hand tools, the resulting debris is burned, and then maize is planted for a period from one to three years. The land is then allowed to rest for several years before recultivation.

7. Items (2.01)–(2.03): Adams, 1973a, pp. 24–26; Culbert, 1974, p. 46.

8. Item (2.04): Benson, 1967, p. 126; Sanders, 1973, pp. 328–332; Culbert, 1974, pp. 41–46.

9. Items (2.05)–(2.07): Adams, 1973a, pp. 26, 29, 32; Sanders, 1973, pp. 332–341. See also Cowgill, 1964, p. 153; Saul, 1973, pp. 301–324; Willey, 1973, p. 100.

10. Sabloff and Willey, 1967, p. 316. See also Adams, 1973a, p. 26; Erasmus, 1968, pp. 170–194.

11. Item (2.08): Cowgill, 1964, p. 152; Andrews IV, 1973, pp. 259–260.

12. Sanders, 1973, p. 340.

13. Culbert, for instance, notes that prehistoric South Americans farmed their swamplands by "building ridged-field systems in which dirt is piled up to make ridges that are high enough to avoid destructive amounts of moisture [and that] . . . some [such systems] have been discovered along the Rio Candelaria at the western edge of the Maya lowland" (Culbert, 1973b, p. 49).

14. Items (2.09)–(2.13): Adams, 1973a, p. 26; Culbert, 1973, pp. 71–72; Sanders, 1973, p. 340; Willey and Shimkin, 1973, pp. 474–476, 482–483; Culbert, 1974, pp. 47–49.

15. Items (2.14)–(2.16): Morley and Brainerd, 1956, p. 71; Cowgill, 1964, p. 152; Thompson, 1966, pp. 102–103; Sabloff and Willey, 1967, p. 315.

16. Thompson, 1966, pp. 100–109; and Thompson 1970, pp. 79–83.

17. Items (3.1)–(3.5): Thompson, 1966, pp. 100–109; and Thompson, 1970, pp. 79–83.

18. Sanders, 1973, p. 361.

19. Culbert, 1974, p. 109.

20. Items (3.6)–(3.7): Morley and Brainerd, 1956, pp. 57–73; Gallenkamp, 1959, pp. 158–163; Sabloff and Willey, 1967, pp. 317–318; Adams, 1973a, pp. 29–30; Sabloff, 1973, pp. 37–38; Sanders, 1973, p. 346, 361; and Willey and Shimkin, 1973, pp. 467–468, 485.

21. Cowgill, 1964, p. 154. Items (4.1)–(4.2): Cowgill, 1964, p. 154; Benson, 1967, p. 130–131; Sabloff and Willey, 1967, pp. 319–330; Adams, 1973a, pp. 30–33; Adams, 1973b, pp. 149–158; Sabloff, 1973, pp. 127–129; Webb, 1973, p. 402; Willey and Shimkin, 1973, pp. 464–465, 469–470.

22. Item (4.3): Cowgill, 1964, p. 154.

23. For example, Sanders argues that nutritional deprivation would result at most in "a reduction of population to the point where a viable subsistence system would become reestablished" (Sanders, 1973, p. 364).

24. Items (4.4)–(4.5): Sanders, 1973, pp. 364–365; Willey and Shimkin, 1973, pp. 470–473.

25. Cowgill, 1964, pp. 155–156.

26. Items (4.6)–(4.7): Culbert, 1973b, pp. 89–92; Rands, 1973, p. 197. See also Webb, 1973, p. 368.

27. Arguments are often of more than one of my argument kinds. For instance, all arguments of kind (1) support the conclusion of an argument of kind (2). All arguments of kind (2) support the conclusion of an argument of kind (3), and vice versa.

28. Item (2.03) is one of the few clear exceptions which I discovered to this rule. Culbert, 1974, p. 46. See also the use made by Shimkin of what he calls "comparative evidence," in 1973, pp. 269–299.

29. Other examples include (2.02), (2.04), and (4.1). See also (3.4) and (3.5).

30. Other examples include (2.01), (3.2), (3.3), and (4.2).

31. Other examples include (3.7) and (4.6).

32. Benson, 1967, p. 127. Item (4.5) is another example.

33. Sanders, 1973, p. 340. For additional examples, see Cowgill, 1964, p. 152; Sabloff and Willey, 1967, p. 315; Culbert, 1974, pp. 47–49. Perhaps (4.7) is another example.

34. As we shall see, the logic of explanatory controversy in historical studies is not only comparative, it is holistic. Local explanatory disagreements and larger interpretational disagreements are intertwined. This affects how one argues both for explanans and explanandum. But this complication is best postponed until after discussion of the taxonomy of arguments.

35. Sanders, 1973, pp. 334, 362.

36. Shimkin, 1973, pp. 269–299. Other examples include (2.05) and Saul, 1973.

37. Perhaps (2.13), (2.14), and (2.15) are negative arguments of kind (2). Some archaeologists suggest (see 2.16) that because something unknown, but not including subsistence failure, was responsible for the collapse of a few of the earliest centers to collapse, and subsistence failure can be shown via negative arguments of kind (3) not to be a sufficient explanation of the collapse of any center, this unknown something may be a sufficient explanation of the collapse even of those centers where subsistence failure is present, and subsistence failure may not even be a partial explanation of the collapse of any center. This line, which may be construed to include either a positive argument of kind (3) or a negative argument of kind (2), is curious in that it is not an argument for a particular favored explanation, since it is not known what that explanation is, but rather an argument for some favored explanation or other that does not include subsistence failure among its explanatory facts.

38. For additional examples, see Cowgill, 1964, pp. 152, 154.

39. Andrews, 1973, pp. 259–260. For additional examples, see notes 5 and 11.

40. Sanders, 1973, p. 364. For an additional example, see Thompson, 1966, p. 104.

41. Sanders, 1973. For additional examples, see Cowgill, 1964, pp. 145–159; Adams, 1973b, pp. 149–158.

42. The idea that we must evaluate competing explanations holistically bears interesting similarities to the related idea of "universal hermeneutics." See, for instance, Taylor, 1980, pp. 25–38, and Makkreel, 1986, pp. 1–19.

43. I am relying here and in my following summaries of explanations on Runyan, 1982, pp. 38–40.

44. Murphey, 1973, p. 111.

45. Runyan also raises this question. See Runyan, 1982, p. 42.

46. Some philosophers—see, for instance, Harman, 1986, pp. 67–68—suggest that explanations do not compete unless they are comparably specific and/or of the same "type" or "level." But it is unclear whether this is true—see, for instance, note 37 above—and, even if it is true, unclear what is meant by "comparably specific," or "type," or "level."

4: CAUSAL WEIGHTING

1. Carr, 1962, p. 117.

2. Hexter, 1978, p. 30.

3. Barzun and Graff, 1977, p. 145.

4. Stone, 1972, p. 58.

5. Nagel, 1961, p. 587. Compare with Nagel's remarks on pp. 588–592, which have a different tone.

6. Dray, 1964, pp. 47–58, and 1978. See also Stretton, 1969, and McCullagh, 1971 and 1984.

7. Dray, 1978, pp. 168–169.

8. Dray, 1964, pp. 47–58. See also Dray's treatment of Hinsley's remarks, in Dray, 1978, p. 174.

9. M. White, 1965, pp. 106, 129.

10. Ducasse, 1924, pp. 19–20, and 1966, pp. 238–241; Feinberg, 1964, pp. 29–47, 55–61; Gorovitz, 1965, pp. 695–711, and 1969, pp. 61–72; Hart and Honoré, 1959, pp. 30–40; Scriven, 1966, pp. 238–264; Shope, 1967, pp. 312–320; and M. White, 1965, pp. 105–181.

11. Some theorists distinguish explanatory from attributive causal inquiries, depending on whether the main purpose of the inquiry is to explain or to attribute responsibility, and then claim that their accounts are applicable only to explanatory causal inquiries. See, for instance, Hart and Honoré, 1959, pp. 22–23, Feinberg, 1964, pp. 58–59, and Scriven, 1966, p. 262, n.9. M. White, who does not rely on this distinction, admits certain "moralistic exceptions" to his account. See M. White, 1965, pp. 116–117. Such a qualification on the consensus account may be

necessary, but there are many attributive inquiries—see, for instance, Dray, 1978, pp. 161–163—in which it does not seem to be.

12. Jones's earlier views are in Jones, 1955.

13. Jones, 1964, pp. 1026–1027, emphasis added.

14. Jones, 1966, p. 370.

15. See Alexander, 1966, for a similar criticism of Jones.

16. Jones, 1964, pp. 1067–1068.

17. Jones, 1964, p. 1067.

18. Jones, 1964, p. 1027.

19. Jones, 1964, p. 1032.

20. Jones, 1964, p. 1047.

21. Jones, 1964, p. 1048.

22. Analysis (D2) closely resembles a proposal made by Hammond, which may, in turn, have been based partly on an earlier proposal of my own. See Hammond, 1977, pp. 103–128.

23. See, for instance, Mackie, 1974, pp. 29–87.

24. See, for instance, Pastin, 1977.

25. Pork, 1985, is an interesting and suggestive study of how historians who are arguing in contexts where statistical techniques are inapplicable attempt to justify counterfactuals. Note especially the role of negative arguments of kind (3) in the arguments he surveys.

26. Such quantitative assessments are, of course, quite common in economic history. See, for instance, Fogel, 1964, and also the discussions in McClelland, 1975, pp. 153–161, and McCullagh, 1984, pp. 194–202.

5: CONCEPTUAL AND EMPIRICAL SUBJECTIVISM

1. Dray, 1964, pp. 22–23.

2. See, for example, M. White, 1949; Meldin, 1952; Passmore, 1958; Nagel, 1961, chap. 13; Mandelbaum, 1963; and Atkinson, 1978, chap. 3.

3. Some historians apparently think it legitimate to subordinate descriptive and explanatory to moral or political or aesthetic objectives. David Hollinger, for instance, claims that "the entire notion of intersubjective validity in history must live alongside the suspicion, if not the conviction, that the knowledge-producing aim of history is secondary to, or in any case qualified by, the moral and aesthetic aims that presumably distinguish it from all sciences, physical and social" (Hollinger, 1973, p. 383). See also Zinn, 1970, chap. 20. For a contrary view, see Hexter, 1971, pp. 73–74, 146–147, 229, and 240.

4. Dray, 1962a, 1964. Compare McCullaugh, 1971, pp. 215–229, and Stretton, 1969, pp. 48–72, 135–141, 300–364.

5. Dray, 1964, p. 55.

6. Dray, 1964, pp. 51–52.

7. Consider a second example. In Dray, 1962b, Dray argues that what he calls "a descriptive, period history," is necessarily subjective. (See also,

Dray, 1964, pp. 29–32, and 1967, pp. 26–30, where the argument is repeated.) Dray does not define "descriptive, period history," but instead distinguishes through examples between what he calls "explanatory history" and "descriptive history," citing Gibbon's *Decline and Fall of the Roman Empire* as an example of an explanatory historical study, and G. M. Young's *Victorian England: Portrait of an Age* and Carlton Hayes's *Generation of Materialism* as examples of descriptive historical studies. Dray further distinguishes between two kinds of descriptive historical studies, "theme" historical studies and "period" historical studies, citing G. M. Trevelyan's *The English Revolution* as an example of a theme historical study and the works of Young and Hayes already mentioned as examples of period historical studies. Dray's basis for his distinction between theme and period historcal studies is that a theme historical study "has a subject determined by the sort of unity which makes us call it a single event, movement, state of affairs, etc.," whereas the subject of a period historical study "is determined chiefly by spatiotemporal criteria" (Dray, 1962b, p. 223). Dray claims only that descriptive, period historical studies are necessarily subjective. I shall use the expression, "period study," in what follows, to mean "descriptive period historical study."

Dray's argument that period studies are necessarily subjective may be formulated as follows:

(8) It is necessarily the case that something is a period study only if it is based on an evaluative criterion of selection.

(9) It is necessarily the case that something is based on an evaluative criterion of selection only if it is subjective.

Therefore, (10) it is necessarily the case that something is a period study only if it is subjective.

The argument is clearly valid, but is it sound? Dray assumes that (9) is definitionally true, and does not argue for it. He does argue for (8), but his argument suggests that he does not understand that (8) is true only if it also is definitionally true.

Dray begins his argument for (8) by sketching the positivist theory of historical explanation, which he does not accept, in order to contrast the possibilities available for explanatory and descriptive histories.

> Let me admit, however, that if the above-mentioned account of what it is to explain something *were* accepted by historians, then there would be a non-evaluative criterion of selection for explanatory histories. [But] . . . no similar solution of the problem is *possible* in the case of *descriptive* histories. It may, of course, be unrealistic in practice to expect historians, in offering explanations, to outline sets of jointly sufficient conditions; but the notion of such a set does at least offer an ideal of objective selection which could *conceivably* be realized. There is no corresponding ideal of selection for descriptive histories which could

conceivably be realized. For the only candidate would appear to be the notion of a "complete description." And this is something which it is in principle impossible to give (Dray, 1962b, p. 219).

Dray does not say whether an explanatory historical study written according to the criterion of selection implicit in the positivist theory of historical explanation would be subject to criticism, given the standards that historians now employ to evaluate such studies. One can easily imagine that it would be. No matter. An alternative criterion of selection for explanatory historical studies—that implicit in the positivist theory—is at least conceivable. So, historians could presumably fashion new standards of evaluation for judging historical studies written in accordance with such a criterion. According to Dray, period studies are different.

Dray makes two claims about period studies. First, that "the problem" of the period historian is "to relate the *significant* or *important* things which happened" in the period under investigation. And secondly, that there is no criterion of importance which is non-evaluative. But consider: Could something be a period study, albeit a bad period study, even though it did not relate the important things which happened in the period under investigation? And, could something be a period study even though it was written in accordance with a non-evaluative principle of selection? Dray does not explicitly address either question, but if his argument to show that period studies are necessarily evaluative is sound, then the answer to both questions must be no.

Dray argues for his claim that the problem for those who write period historical studies is to state the important things which happened during the period under investigation.

> That historians really do accept such a tougher obligation is shown by their recognition of the legitimacy of a comparison between two differing accounts of the same subject, in terms of the "adequacy" of each. One can certainly be judged "better" than the other, and one can be so bad, without containing any false statements, that it becomes distorted; it no longer gives a "true picture" (Dray, 1962b, pp. 220–221).

But such considerations show only that period studies are as a matter of fact evaluative, not that they are necessarily evaluative, hence not that premise (8) is true. To show that there could not be a non-evaluative criterion of selection for period studies, Dray would have to argue on the basis of definitions of "period study" and "important."

Dray's confusion about what it takes to establish that there could not be a non-evaluative criterion of importance for period studies is especially striking since he concedes, for the sake of argument, that there could be a non-evaluative "causal" criterion of importance. (Dray, 1962b, p. 221). But, Dray cannot possibly establish his conclusion that period studies are necessarily evaluative, and hence necessarily subjective, if he makes such a concession. How then does he try?

Dray argues that a period historian who did not mention certain events, even if they were not causally important, would be subject to criticism by other historians. (See Dray, 1962b, pp. 221–222). But this does not show that there could not be a non-evaluative criterion of selection for period studies.

Dray's arguments are appropriate to establishing that period studies are in fact evaluative, or perhaps, that period studies are ordinarily judged in terms of evaluative criteria of importance. His arguments for these conclusions are important since they make explicit what is implicit in historical practice and thereby increase our understanding of the way historical studies actually work, and thereby pave the way for possible methodological reform.

Dray argues from the fact that period studies are evaluative to the conclusion that they must be, that is, he argues on the basis of empirical evidence for conceptual subjectivism. But empirical evidence is irrelevant to the justification of conceptual subjectivism, not just in the case of Dray's two arguments, but always.

I have focused on Dray's work because he more than any other highly visible analytic philosopher has done philosophy of history in the ways I have been arguing in this book that it should be done. Nevertheless, in each of the two arguments I considered, Dray first does important work in empirical philosophy of history and then misconstrues what he has done as an exercise in conceptual philosophy of history. Understanding how Dray gets confused, and why his work is nevertheless valuable, may help to wean us away from our preoccupation with the question of whether historical studies are necessarily subjective.

8. For an indication of the extent to which there has been confusion and disagreement over the role of historical evidence in the justification of scientific subjectivism, see Lakatos and Musgrave, 1970, pp. 19–22, 49–50, 55–58, 66–75, 115–122, 138, 178–180, 198–199, 214–219, and 235–241.

9. Scheffler, [1967] 1982, p. 74.

10. Scheffler, [1967] 1982, p. 126. The charge that subjectivism is self-refuting is not confined to the discussion of historical studies and science, but arises predictably almost every time any sweeping form of relativism is considered. Charles Guignon, for instance, in a critique of Heidegger's views, argues that "the relativist seems to be caught in a dilemma. If relativism is true, then our thoughts about other cultures and languages can make sense only within the framework of our own language, in which case one cannot coherently work out the relativist thesis. On the other hand, if relativism makes sense and a case can be made for it, then it must be false, since one *can*, in fact, transcend one's own world-view in order to comprehend other views" (Guignon, 1983, pp. 211–212). Clearly the view that subjectivist and relativist arguments are necessarily self-refuting is nearly as persistent as subjectivism and relativism themselves.

11. For instance, the historian Vernon Parrington once characterized the American frontiersman Davy Crockett as "first among the Smart Alecks of the canebrakes."

12. Mackie, 1965, p. 263.

13. Quoted by Nagel, 1963, p. 81, from Carr, 1963, p. 54.

14. Nagel, 1963, p. 82, emphasis added.

15. Hook, 1963, pp. 258–259.

16. An important motive for thinking that certain arguments for skepticism are self-refuting is that many of the most influential skeptics have been historians whose professional behavior seems to betray their commitment to views incompatible with their skepticism. For example, the historian Cushing Strout has remarked of Becker and Beard that "insofar as both men aimed to provide more adequate explanations of historical change, their practice of history conflicted, to this extent, with their philosophies of skeptical relativism" (Strout, 1958, p. 65). Compare Hexter, 1972, p. 254. Surprisingly, Beard himself sometimes wrote as if he agreed, once remarking that "the apostle of relativity is destined to be destroyed by the child of his own brain" (Beard, 1934, p. 147). But these are not good reasons for thinking that arguments for skepticism are necessarily self-refuting. To see this we need not even agree with the defense of skepticism presented above; it is enough simply to distinguish between arguments for skepticism, on the one hand, and the more inclusive views of skeptics, on the other. That many skeptics hold views incompatible with their skepticism may be of historical or psychological interest, but it hardly refutes skepticism. There is more than one way to resolve a contradiction.

17. See, for instance, Kuhn, [1962] 1970, p. 262.

18. See, for instance, Dray, 1964, p. 40.

19. Strong empirical subjectivism, for instance, would insure not only that historical studies *always have been* subjective, but also that had a historical study been composed on some occasion when none was, it *would have been* subjective, and not only that historical studies always *will be* subjective, but also that were a historical study composed on some occasion when none will be, it *would be* subjective.

20. An example of the former is Carr's discussion of Gibbon in Carr, 1962, pp. 105f.; of the latter, Mannheim's discussion, in his analysis of conservative thought in Germany in the first half of the nineteenth century, of the "authentic conservativism" of the erstwhile historian, Justus Möser. Mannheim, 1953, pp. 74–164.

21. Connolly, 1967, p. 75; Shils, 1974, p. 86.

6: MODEST EMPIRICAL SUBJECTIVISM

1. See, for example, Abel, [1948] 1953, pp. 677–687, 1975, pp. 99–102; Nagel, 1961, pp. 482–484; Hempel, [1948] 1965, pp. 245–295; Rudner, 1966, p. 73; and Van Evra, 1971, pp. 377–381.

2. Abel, [1948] 1953, p. 679. Page numbers here and below are to the Feigl and Brodbeck reprinted edition of 1953.

3. Abel, [1948] 1953, p. 679.

4. Abel, [1948] 1953, p. 680.

5. Abel, [1948] 1953, p. 683.

6. Abel, [1948] 1953, p. 687, emphasis added.

7. Abel, [1948] 1953, p. 685.

8. Farmer, 1964, contains a fascinating history of the debate over the Synoptic Problem.

9. Abbott's argument is quoted in Farmer, 1964, p. 75.

10. Farmer, 1964, p. 77.

11. Streeter, 1924, p. 163.

12. Styler, 1966, p. 230.

13. Streeter, 1924, p. 158.

14. Kümmel, 1966, p. 50.

15. Kümmel, 1966, p. 50.

16. Kümmel, 1966, p. 47.

17. Kümmel, 1966, p. 47.

18. Styler, 1966, p. 229.

19. Compare the related argument in Cohen, 1973.

20. Compare the related argument in Van Evra, 1971.

21. Scriven, 1971. See also, Nozick, 1981, pp. 636–637, and McCullagh, 1984, pp. 72–73.

22. Berlin, 1966, p. 50.

23. Consider, for instance, the dispute between Geoffrey Elton and J. H. Hexter over the significance of the so-called "Apology of the House of Commons" of 1604 to the question of how one should interpret the events preceding the English Civil War. Elton, 1966, pp. 330–334, and Hexter, 1978, pp. 30–50. See also, Dray, 1987, p. 142.

APPENDIX

1. Levich, 1965, p. 348, so far as I know, is the sole exception. He noticed what I call "historical counterexamples" and also their philosophical significance. But his brief discussion, buried in a book review, seems to have had no impact on the debate over the positivist analysis. Fischer, 1971, pp. 178–180, noticed historical counterexamples, and argued that they are fallacious. (See note 5, below.) M. White, 1965, pp. 64–66, came close to noticing historical counterexamples, but did not recognize their role in the defense of historical explanations.

2. Davidson, in 1967, was the first to dwell on the importance of the distinction between "sufficient cause" and "sufficient causal explanation." He would understand statements of the form, "p is a sufficient cause of q," where p and q are replaced by full sentences in the indicative mood, as saying that "p is a sufficient *causal explanation* of q." See Davidson, 1967, pp. 691–703. I agree with Davidson. But to conform more

closely to language familiar to historians and to thereby make this Appendix less technical and more readable, I have not followed Davidson's way of expressing his distinctions. My arguments can be amended easily to accommodate Davidson's point.

3. Other examples include: Andrews, 1973, pp. 259–260; Beale, 1946, pp. 81, 84, 90; Benson, 1972, p. 181; Bloch, 1961, p. 35; Koenigsberger, 1972, p. 396; Pierson, 1972, pp. 74, 89; Samuelsson, 1973, p. 122; Saunders, 1963, pp. 4, 8, 9, 17; Stone, 1965, p. 175; and Strout, 1965, p. 88.

4. There is a variation on Argument (B) which may also deserve to be called a basic historical counterexample. Premise (1) remains the same. For (3), substitute (3.1): The fact that *this flood* was a flood was not a sufficient cause of the fact that *this famine* was a famine. The expressions, "this flood," and "this famine," unlike any expressions in (3), refer uniquely to particular events.

5. D. H. Fischer seems to have had a similar objection in mind when he responded to Bury's quoted remarks: "But this is a mistake. The three causal elements which Bury rejects may have interacted with each other, and with still other elements, in such a way as to produce very different results in the West and the East" (Fischer, 1971, p. 179).

6. The other form of basic historical counterexample, mentioned above in note 4, has a slightly different form. (BHC2): Premise (11) remains the same. For (12), substitute (12.1): the mere fact that c was α was not a sufficient cause of the fact that e was β. The letters, c and e, in (12.1), are placeholders for terms, such as "this flood," which refer uniquely to particular events.

BIBLIOGRAPHY

Abel, T. 1948. The Operation Called *Verstehen*. *American Journal of Sociology* 54:211–218. Reprinted in Feigl and Brodbeck 1953 677–687.

Abel, T. 1975. *Verstehen I* and *Verstehen II*. *Theory and Decision* 6:99–102.

Adams, R.E.W. 1973a. The Collapse of Maya Civilization: A Review of Previous Theories. In Culbert 1973a, 21–34.

Adams, R.E.W. 1973b. Maya Collapse: Transformation and Termination in the Ceramic Sequence at Altar de Sacrificios. In Culbert 1973a, 133–163.

Alexander, Paul. 1966. Review of A.H.M. Jones, *The Later Roman Empire, 184–602. American Journal of Philology* 87:337–350.

Andrews IV, E. W. 1973. The Development of Maya Civilization After Abandonment of Southern Cities. In Culbert 1973a, 243–265.

Atkinson, R. F. 1978. *Knowledge and Explanation in History*. Ithaca: Cornell University Press.

Barzun, J., and H. F. Graff. 1977. *The Modern Researcher*. 3d ed. New York: Harcourt, Brace, Jovanovich, Inc.

Beale, H. K. 1946. What Historians Have Said about the Causes of the Civil War. In Social Science Research Council, *Theory and Practice in Historical Study: A Report of the Committee on Historiography*. New York: Social Science Research Council, 55–102.

Beard, Charles. 1934. Written History as an Act of Faith. *The American Historical Review* 39: 219–229. Reprinted in Meyerhoff 1959, 140–151.

Benson, E. P. 1967. *The Maya World*. New York: Thomas Y. Crowell.

Benson, Lee. 1972. *Toward the Scientific Study of History*. Philadelphia: Lippincott.

Berlin, I. 1960. History and Theory: The Concept of Scientific History. *History and Theory* 1:1–31. Reprinted in Dray 1966, 5–53.

Billington, Ray, ed. 1966. *The Frontier Thesis*. New York: Holt, Rinehart and Winston.

Reprinted versions of the source have been used for page references in all cases when reprint publication information is provided in the Bibliography.

Bloch, Marc. 1961. *Feudal Society*. Chicago: University of Chicago Press.

Braudel, Fernand. 1972. *The Mediterranean and the Mediterranean World in the Age of Philip II*. Translated by Sian Reynolds. 2d ed. 2 vols. New York: Harper and Row.

Bury, J. B. 1958. *History of the Later Roman Empire*. 2 vols. New York: Dover Publications.

Canary, R. H., and H. Kozicki, eds. 1978 *The Writing of History: Literary Form and Historical Understanding*. Madison: The University of Wisconsin Press.

Capitan, W., and D. Merrill, eds. 1964. *Metaphysics and Explanation*. Pittsburgh: University of Pittsburgh Press.

Carr, E. H. 1962. *What Is History?* New York: Alfred A. Knopf.

Carter, C. H., ed. 1966. *From the Renaissance to the Counter-Reformation* London: Cape.

Cohen, H. 1973. *Das Verstehen* and Historical Knowledge. *American Philosophical Quarterly* 10:299–306.

Collingwood, R. G. 1946. *The Idea of History*. Oxford: Clarendon Press.

Connolly, William. 1967. *Political Science and Ideology*. New York: Atherton Press.

Cowgill, G. L. 1964. The End of Classic Maya Culture: A Review of Recent Evidence. *Southwestern Journal of Anthropology* 20:145–159.

Culbert, T. P. 1973a. *The Classic Maya Collapse*. Albuquerque: University of New Mexico Press.

Culbert, T. P. 1973b. The Maya Downfall at Tikal. In Culbert 1973a, 63–92.

Culbert, T. P. 1974. *The Lost Civilization*. New York: Harper and Row.

Curry, R. O. 1973. *The Abolitionists*. New York: Dryden.

Davidson, D. 1967. Causal Relations. *Journal of Philosophy* 64: 691–703.

Davidson, D. 1978. Comments: Is Philosophy of History Possible? In Yovel 1978, 235–236.

Donagan, Alan. 1969. Alternative Historical Explanations and Their Verification. *The Monist* 53:58–89.

Dray, William. 1962a. Some Causal Accounts of the American Civil War. *Daedalus* 91:578–592.

Dray, William. 1962b. The Historian's Problem of Selection. In Nagel 1962, 595–603. Reprinted in Nash 1969, 2:216–227.

Dray, William. 1964. *Philosophy of History*. Englewood Cliffs, N.J.: Prentice-Hall.

Dray, William, ed. 1966. *Philosophical Analysis and History*. New York: Harper and Row.

Dray, William. 1967. History and Value Judgments. In Edwards 1967, 4:26–30.

Dray, William. 1978. Concepts of Causation in A.J.P. Taylor's Account of the Second World War. *History and Theory* 17:149–174.

Dray, William. 1987. J. H. Hexter, Neo-Whiggism and Early Stuart Historiography. *History and Theory* 26:133–149.

Ducasse, C. J. 1924. *Causation and the Types of Necessity.* Seattle: University
of Washington Press.

Ducasse, C. J. 1966. "Cause" and "Condition". *Journal of Philosophy*
63:238–241.

Edwards, Paul, ed. 1967. *The Encyclopedia of Philosophy.* 8 vols. New York:
Macmillan.

Elton, G. 1966. A High Road to Civil War. In Carter 1966, 325–347.

Erasmus, C. J. 1968. Thoughts on Upward Collapse: An Essay on Explanation in Anthropology. *Southwestern Journal of Anthropology*
24:170–194.

Farmer, W. R. 1964. *The Synoptic Problem.* New York: Macmillan.

Feigl, H., and M. Brodbeck, eds. 1953. *Readings in the Philosophy of Science.*
New York: Appleton, Century, Crofts.

Feinberg, J. 1964. Causing Voluntary Actions. In Capitan and Merrill
1964, 29–47, 55–61.

Fischer, D. H. 1971. *Historian's Fallacies.* London: Routledge and Kegan
Paul.

Fogel, R. W. 1964. *Railroads and American Economic Growth: Essays in
Econometric History.* Baltimore: Johns Hopkins University Press.

Gallenkamp, C. 1959. *Maya: The Riddle and Rediscovery of a Lost Civilization.* New York: Mackay.

Geyl, P. 1956. Toynbee's System of Civilizations. In Montagu 1956, 39–
72.

Giere, R. N. 1984. *Understanding Scientific Reasoning.* 2d ed. New York:
Holt, Rinehart and Winston.

Glynn, Simon, ed. 1986. *European Philosophy and the Human and Social
Sciences.* Aldershot, Hampshire, England: Gower Publishing
Co., Ltd.

Gorman, J. L. 1982. *The Expression of Historical Knowledge* Edinburgh:
Edinburgh University Press.

Gorovitz, S. 1965. Causal Judgments and Causal Explanations. *Journal of
Philosophy* 62:695–711.

Gorovitz, S. 1969. Aspects of the Pragmatics of Explanation. *Nous* 3:61–
72.

Green, R. W., ed. 1973. *Protestantism, Capitalism and Social Science.* 2d ed.
Lexington, Mass.: Heath.

Guignon, Charles. 1983. *Heidegger and the Problem of Knowledge.* Indianapolis: Hackett Publishing Co.

Hammond, M. 1977. Weighting Causes in Historical Explanation. *Theo-
ria* 43:103–128.

Harman, Gilbert. 1986. *Change in View.* Cambridge: MIT Press.

Hart, H., and A. Honoré. 1959. *Causation in the Law.* Oxford: Oxford
University Press.

Hempel, C. R. 1942. The Function of General Laws in History. *Journal of Philosophy* 39:35–48. Reprinted, with some changes, in Hempel 1965, 231–243.

Hempel, C. R. 1948. Studies in the Logic of Explanation. *Philosophy of Science* 15:135–175. Reprinted, with some changes, in Hempel 1965, 245–295.

Hempel, C. R. 1965 *Aspects of Scientific Explanation.* New York: The Free Press.

Hexter, J. H. 1971. *The History Primer.* New York: Basic Books.

Hexter, J. H. 1978. Power Struggle, Parliament and Liberty in Early Stuart England. *Journal of Modern History* 50:1–50.

Hofstadter, Richard. 1966. The Thesis Disputed. In Billington 1966, 102–108.

Hollinger, David, 1973. T. S. Kuhn's Theory of Science and Its Implications for History. *The American Historical Review* 18:370–393.

Hook, Sidney. 1963a. Objectivity and Reconstruction in History. In Hook 1963b, 250–274.

Hook, Sidney, ed. 1963b *Philosophy and History.* New York: New York University Press.

Jones, A.H.M. 1955. The Decline and Fall of the Roman Empire. *History* n.s. 40:209–226.

Jones, A.H.M. 1964. *The Later Roman Empire, 284–602.* 2 vols. Norman, Oklahoma: University of Oklahoma Press.

Jones, A.H.M. 1966. *The Decline of the Ancient World.* London: Longmans.

Kaplan, Abraham. 1978. Historical Interpretation. In Yovel 1978, 27–37.

Koenigsberger, H. G. 1972. Revolutionary Conclusions. *History* 57:394–398.

Kuhn, Thomas. [1962] 1970. *The Structure of Scientific Revolutions.* 2d ed. Chicago: University of Chicago Press.

Kuhn, Thomas. 1970. Reflections on my Critics. In Lakatos and Musgrave 1970, 231–278.

Kümmel, W. G., ed. 1966. *Introduction to the New Testament,* founded by Paul Feine and Johannes Behm, 14th ed. Nashville, Tenn.: Abingdon Press.

Lakatos, Imre and Alan Musgrave, eds. 1970. *Criticism and the Growth of Knowledge.* Cambridge: Cambridge University Press.

Levich, Marvin. 1965. Review of S. Hook, ed. *Philosophy and History. History and Theory* 4:328–349.

McClelland, P. D. 1975. *Causal Explanation and Model Building in History, Economics, and the New Economic History.* Ithaca: Cornell University Press.

McCullagh, C. Behan. 1971. Interpretation in History. *Australian Journal of Politics and History* 17:215–229.

McCullagh, C. Behan. 1984. *Justifying Historical Descriptions.* Cambridge: Cambridge University Press.

Mackie, J. L. 1965. Causes and Conditions. *American Philosophical Quarterly* 2:245–264.

Mackie, J. L. 1974. *The Cement of the Universe.* Oxford: Oxford University Press.

MacKie, E. W. 1961. New Light on the End of Classic Maya Culture of Benque Viejo, British Honduras. *American Antiquity* 27:216–224.

Makkreel, R. A. 1986. Dilthey and Universal Hermeneutics: The Status of the Human Sciences. In Glynn 1986, 1–19.

Mandelbaum, M. 1963. Objectivism in History. In Hook 1963b, 43–56.

Mandelbaum, M. 1977. *The Anatomy of Historical Knowledge.* Baltimore: The Johns Hopkins University Press.

Mannheim, Karl. 1953. *Essays on Sociology and Social Psychology.* New York: Oxford University Press.

Martin, Raymond. 1979. Historical Counterexamples and Sufficient Cause. *Mind* 88:59–73.

Martin, Raymond. 1979. History and Subjectivity. *Ratio* 21:44–62.

Martin, Raymond. 1980. Explanatory Controversy in Historical Studies. A Case Study: The Classic Maya Collapse. In van Inwagen 1980, 219–235.

Martin, Raymond. 1981. Beyond Positivism: A Research Program for Philosophy of History. *Philosophy of Science* 48:112–121.

Martin, Raymond. 1982. Causes, Conditions and Causal Importance. *History and Theory* 21:53–74.

Martin, Raymond. 1985. History and the Brewmaster's Nose. *Canadian Journal of Philosophy* 15:253–272.

Meldin, A. I. 1952. Historical Objectivity, A "Noble Dream." *The Journal of General Education* 7:17–24. Reprinted in Nash 1969, 2:193–205.

Meyerhoff, Hans, ed. 1959. *The Philosophy of History in Our Time.* New York: Doubleday.

Mink, Louis. 1978. Narrative Form as a Cognitive Instrument. In Canary and Kozicki 1978, 129–149.

Montagu, M. F. Ashley, ed. 1956. *Toynbee and History.* Boston: Portor Sargent.

Morley, S. G., and G. W. Brainerd. 1956. *The Ancient Maya.* 3d ed. Stanford: Stanford University Press.

Moule, C.F.D. 1966. *The Birth of the New Testament.* 2d ed. London: Adams and Charles Black.

Murphey, M. 1973. *Our Knowledge of the Historical Past,* Indianapolis: Bobbs-Merrill.

Nadel, G. H., ed. 1965. *Studies in the Philosophy of History.* New York: Harper and Row.

Nagel, Ernest. 1961. *The Structure of Science.* New York: Harcourt, Brace and World.

Nagel, Ernest, P. Suppes, and A. Tarski, eds. 1962. *Logic, Methodology, and Philosophy of Science.* Stanford: Stanford University Press.

Nagel, Ernest. 1963. Relativism and Some Problems of Working Histori-
    ans. In Hook 1963, 76–91.
Nash, R. H., ed. 1969. *Ideas of History*. 2 vols. New York: E. P. Dutton &
    Co.
Nozick, Robert. 1981. *Philosophical Explanations*. Cambridge: Harvard
    University Press.
Pastin, Mark. 1977. Counterfactuals in Epistemology. *Synthese* 34:479–
    495.
Passmore, John. 1958. The Objectivity of History. *Philosophy* 33:97–111.
    Reprinted in Dray 1966, 75–94.
Pierson, G. W. 1972. The Frontier and American Institutions: A Criti-
    cism of the Turner Theory. In G. R. Taylor 1972, 70–97.
Pirenne, Henri. 1931. What Are Historians Trying to Do?. In Rice 1931,
    435–445. Reprinted in Meyerhoff 1959, 87–99.
Pork, Andrus. 1985. Assessing Relative Causal Importance in History.
    History and Theory 24:62–69.
Rands, R. L. 1973. The Classic Maya Collapse: Usumacinta Zone and the
    Northwestern Periphery. In Culbert 1973a, 165–205.
Rice, Stuart, ed. 1931. *Methods in Social Science*. Chicago: University of
    Chicago Press.
Rudner, R. 1966. *Philosophy of Social Science*. Englewood Cliffs, N.J.:
    Prentice-Hall.
Runyan, William. 1982. *Life Histories and Psychobiography*. New York: Ox-
    ford University Press.
Sabloff, J. A., and G. R. Willey. 1967. The Collapse of Maya Civilization
    in Southern Lowlands: A Consideration of History and Process.
    Southwestern Journal of Anthropology 23:311–336.
Sabloff, J. A. 1973a. Major Themes in the Past Hypotheses of the Maya
    Collapse. In Culbert 1973a, 35–40.
Sabloff, J. A. 1973b. Continuity and Disruption During Terminal Late
    Classic Times at Siebal. In Culbert 1973a, 107–131.
Samuelsson, Kurt. 1973. Religion and Economic Action. In R. W. Green
    1973, 106–137.
Sanders, W. T. 1973. The Cultural Ecology of the Lowland Maya: A
    Reevaluation. In T. P. Culbert 1973a, 325–365.
Saul, F. B. 1973. Disease in the Maya Area: The Pre-Columbian Evi-
    dence. In Culbert 1973a, 301–324.
Saunders, J. J. 1963. The Debate on the Fall of Rome. *History* 48:1–17.
Scheffler, Israel. [1967] 1982. *Science and Subjectivity*. 2d ed. Indianapolis:
    Bobbs-Merrill.
Scheffler, Israel. 1972. Vision and Revolution: A Postscript on Kuhn.
    Philosophy of Science 39:366–374.
Scriven, M. 1966. Causes, Connections and Conditions in History. In
    Dray 1966, 238–264.
Scriven, M. 1971. *Verstehen* Again. *Theory and Decision* 1:382–386.

Shils, Edward. 1974. *Ideology and Utopia* by Karl Mannheim. *Daedalus* 103:83–89.

Shimkin, D. B. 1973. Models for the Downfall: Some Ecological and Culture-Historical Considerations. In Culbert 1973a, 269–299.

Shope, R. 1967. Explanations in Terms of "The Cause." *Journal of Philosophy* 64:312–320.

Skotheim, R. T. 1973. The "Status Revolution" Thesis Criticized. In Curry 1973, 47–51.

Stone, Lawrence. 1965. *Crisis of the Aristocracy, 1558–1641*. Oxford: Oxford University Press.

Stone, Lawrence. 1972. *The Causes of the English Revolution, 1529–1642*. New York: Harper and Row.

Streeter, B. H. 1924. *The Four Gospels*. New York: Macmillan.

Stretton, H. 1969. *The Political Sciences*. London: Routledge and Kegan Paul.

Strout, Cushing. 1958. *The Pragmatic Revolt in American History*. New Haven: Yale University Press.

Strout, Cushing. 1965. Causation and the American Civil War. In Nadel 1965, 86–98.

Styler, G. M. 1966. Excursus IV: The Priority of Mark. In Moule 1966, 223–232.

Taylor, Charles. 1980. Understanding in the Human Sciences. *Review of Metaphysics* 34:25–38.

Taylor, G. R., ed. 1972. *The Turner Thesis*. 3d ed. Lexington, Mass.: Heath.

Thompson, J.E.S. 1966. *The Rise and Fall of Maya Civilization*. Norman: The University of Oklahoma Press.

Thompson, J.E.S. 1970. *Maya History and Religion*. Norman: The University of Oklahoma Press.

Van Evra, J. 1971. On Scriven on "*Verstehen*." *Theory and Decision* 2:377–381.

van Inwagen, Peter. 1980. *Time and Cause*. Dordrecht, Holland: Reidel.

Vann, Richard. 1987. Louis Mink's Linguistic Turn. *History and Theory* 26:1–14.

Veyne, Paul. 1984. *Writing History*. Translated by M. Moore-Rinvolucri. Middletown: Wesleyan University Press.

Webb, M. C. 1973. The Peten Maya Decline Viewed in the Perspective of State Formation. In Culbert 1973a, 367–404.

White, Hayden. 1973. *Metahistory*. Baltimore: Johns Hopkins University Press.

White, Hayden. 1984. The Question of Narrative in Contemporary Historical Theory. *History and Theory* 23:1–33.

White, Morton. 1949. *Social Thought in America*. New York: Viking Press. Reprinted, in part, as Can History Be Objective? Meyerhoff 1959, 188–202.

White, Morton. 1965. *Foundations of Historical Knowledge*. New York: Harper and Row.

Willey, G. R. 1973. Certain Aspects of the Late Classic to Postclassic Periods in the Belize Valley. In Culbert 1973a, 93–106.

Willey, G. R., and D. B. Shimkin. 1973. The Maya Collapse: A Summary View. In Culbert 1973a, 457–501.

Yovel, Yirmiahu, ed. 1978. *Philosophy of History and Action*. Dordrecht: D. Reidel Publishing Co.

Zinn, H. 1970. *The Politics of History*. Boston: Beacon Press.

INDEX